GREAT BRITONS

But be not afraid of greatness: some men
are born great, some achieve greatness,
and some have greatness thrust upon them.

Shakespeare, *Twelfth Night* (1601) act 2, sc. 5

Great Britons

THE GREAT DEBATE

John Cooper

WITH INTRODUCTORY ESSAYS BY

Brian Harrison and Mark Harrison

AND CONTRIBUTIONS FROM

Rosie Boycott, Jeremy Clarkson, Alan Davies,
Richard Holmes, Tristram Hunt, Andrew Marr,
Lucy Moore, Mo Mowlam, Michael Portillo
and Fiona Shaw

NATIONAL PORTRAIT GALLERY

LONDON

Acknowledgements

The authors and publisher are grateful to the following for permission to reproduce copyright material: Oxford English Dictionary of Quotations (OUP); W. H. Auden, *O Love, the interest itself* (the Executors of the Estate, Faber and Faber); Philip Larkin, *Annus Mirabilis* (The Society of Authors); Malcolm Muggeridge, *The Infernal Grove* (The Society of Authors).

The authors and publisher would like to thank the following for assistance in the production of this book:

Rachel Brown, Prof. David Cannadine, Susan George, Prof. Ludmilla Jordonova, Dr David Smith, The Shakespeare Birthplace Trust (www.shakespeare.org.uk), Vicky Robinson, David Wilkinson

The staff and curators of the National Portrait Gallery, London, particularly Pim Baxter, Robert Carr-Archer, John Haywood, Tom Morgan, Jacob Simon, Hazel Sutherland, Pallavi Vadhia

The staff of the BBC including Rachel Budden, Peta Clifton, Jane Root, Sharon Smith and the *Great Britons* production · team (Tom Archer, Ed Bazalgette, Clare Beavan, Alexandra Briscoe, Laura Craig-Gray, Mary Cranitch, Pamela Esterson, Judy Evans, Matt Fisher, Kim Flitcroft, Helen Gibson, Rebecca Hickie, Emma Hindley, Antonia Hinds, John Holdsworth, David Irvine, Laura Jackson, Suzy Jaffe, Sheila Johns, Miriam Jones, Tim Lambert, Michael Lee, Cecile Letourneur, Charlotte Moore, John Mullen, Debbie O'Mahony, Maggie Oakley, John Pendleton, Gerry Pomeroy, Alison Ramsey, Kate Roberts, Kate Smith, Jonathan Stedall, Petra Tauscher, Jessica Taylor, Kate Townsend, Christine Wilson, Simon Winchcombe).

Published in Great Britain by National Portrait Gallery Publications, National Portrait Gallery, St Martin's Place, London WC2H 0HE

For a complete catalogue of current publications, please write to the National Portrait Gallery at the address above, or visit our website at www.npg.org.uk/publications

Views expressed in this publication are not necessarily those held by the Trustees and staff of the National Portrait Gallery or the BBC.

The jacket shows details from the following paintings and photographs: Elizabeth I (1533–1603) attrib. to George Gower, *c.*1588; William Shakespeare (1564–1616) attrib. John Taylor, *c.*1610; Oliver Cromwell (1599–1658) by Robert Walker, *c.*1649; Sir Isaac Newton (1642–1727) by Sir Godfrey Kneller, 1702; Horatio Nelson, Viscount Nelson (1758–1805) by Sir William Beechey, 1800; Isambard Kingdom Brunel (1806–59) by Robert Howlett, 1857; Charles Darwin (1809–82) by Julia Margaret Cameron, 1868; Winston Churchill (1874–1965) by Yousuf Karsh, 1941; John Lennon (1940–80) by Iain MacMillan, 1971; Diana, Princess of Wales (1961–97) by Bryan Organ, 1980. All these paintings and photographs are reproduced in full in the book. Picture credits are listed on page 169.

ISBN pb 1 85514 507 3

A catalogue record for this book is available from the British Library.

PUBLISHING MANAGER: Celia Joicey
CONSULTANT EDITOR: Paul Forty
EDITORIAL ASSISTANT: Kate Martin
PICTURE RESEARCH: Cally Blackman
PRODUCTION: Ruth Müller-Wirth
DESIGN: Philip Lewis

Printed in Italy

Contents

Introduction

The word 'great' is one of the most overused superlatives. And yet the question 'Who do you think is truly great?' is still one that provokes most of us to a very considered, precise and heartfelt reply. There's great; and then there's really Great.

The invitation to the British public to nominate their greatest-ever Briton was initially made by the BBC towards the end of 2001. The subsequent nominations list became the basis for a television series, *Great Britons*; and that series was in turn the inspiration for this book and an accompanying trail at the National Portrait Gallery.

The Great Britons poll took place in November and December 2001. A promotional campaign on BBC ONE, BBC TWO and the BBC website invited people to vote for their greatest-ever Briton. A Briton was defined as 'anyone who was born in the British Isles, including Ireland, or anyone who lived in the British Isles, including Ireland, and who has played a significant part in the life of the British Isles'. The public was able to vote either on-line or by telephone. Mechanisms were set up to identify and dismiss any attempts by individuals or organisations to cast multiple votes.

Despite not initially being related directly to a programme, the poll generated tens of thousands of votes. It was of course impossible to gauge how demographically representative the nominations were. The BBC therefore commissioned a public opinion survey called a Quest Report, a sample of more than 2,000 respondents. Interestingly, the Quest Report nominations almost precisely echoed those of the BBC's general public poll. Eight of the top ten nominations were the same and all the top ten names in the BBC poll appear in the top fifteen of the Quest Report. The Great Britons poll, therefore, appears to be a reasonably true reflection of public opinion.

In creating a television series, BBC TWO decided to commission ten one-hour films, one for each of the top ten nominations as they appeared in the public poll. Each of these top ten Great Britons would be championed by a different presenter acting as their advocate. A summary of the case made by each of these presenters is to be found in this book together with a discussion of the image of each Great Briton by John Cooper, former Head of Education at the National Portrait Gallery.

The aim of the television series was to stimulate national debate over what we value today in our history and culture, and who we want to personify as representative of those values. This book echoes those intentions, but also seeks to carry the discussion further. For the National Portrait Gallery, the BBC series relates closely to certain central ideas. The very shape and extent of the collection in the Gallery is a guide to who and what the British have sought to honour and record. The collection doesn't only pose the question 'Who have been the greatest Britons,' we also ask 'How has their greatness been represented?' The pictorial history of our most famous citizens can be as revealing as their great achievements.

This book therefore explores both the lives of those we now see as great, and the images they have left behind. It features ten people the British public nominated as the greatest Britons of all; and it also examines a further ninety who were nominated in the BBC's Great Britons poll. At the National Portrait Gallery they can be seen in the context of yet another thousand men and women, all with their own claim to fame.

MARK HARRISON
Series Producer for *Great Britons*

JACOB SIMON
Chief Curator,
National Portrait Gallery, London

Our favourite Britons – the top 100

ELIZABETH I
Queen of England and Ireland 1558–1603
English, born Greenwich (1533–1603)

WILLIAM SHAKESPEARE
Dramatist and poet
English, born Stratford-upon-Avon (1564–1616)

OLIVER CROMWELL
Lord Protector 1653–58
English, born Cambridgeshire (1599–1658)

ISAAC NEWTON
Natural philosopher
English, born Grantham, Lincolnshire (1642–1727)

HORATIO NELSON
Vice-admiral
English, born Norfolk (1758–1805)

ISAMBARD KINGDOM BRUNEL
Civil engineer
English, born Portsea, Hampshire (1806–59)

CHARLES DARWIN
Naturalist and originator of the theory of evolution
English, born Shrewsbury, Shropshire (1809–82)

WINSTON CHURCHILL
Prime Minister 1940–45, 1951–55 and author
English, born Blenheim Palace, Oxfordshire 1874–1965

JOHN LENNON
Pop musician; member of The Beatles
English, born Liverpool (1940–80)

DIANA, PRINCESS OF WALES
Princess of Wales
English, born Sandringham, Norfolk (1961–97)

11 ERNEST SHACKLETON
Antarctic explorer
Irish, born Moone, County Kildare (1874–1922)

12 JAMES COOK
Circumnavigator
English, born Marton, Yorkshire (1728–79)

13 ROBERT BADEN POWELL
Founder of the Boy Scouts and Girl Guides
English, born London (1857–1941)

14 ALFRED THE GREAT
King of West-Saxons 871–901
English, born Wantage, Dorset (849–899)

15 ARTHUR WELLESLEY, 1ST DUKE OF WELLINGTON
Field-Marshal and Prime Minister 1828–30
Irish, born Dublin (1769–1852)

16 MARGARET THATCHER
Prime Minister 1979–90
English, born Lincolnshire (1925–)

17 MICHAEL CRAWFORD
Actor and comedian
English, born Isle of Sheppey, Kent (1942–)

18 QUEEN VICTORIA
Queen of the United Kingdom and Ireland 1837–1901
English, born London (1819–1901)

19 PAUL McCARTNEY
Pop musician; member of The Beatles
English, born Liverpool (1942–)

20 ALEXANDER FLEMING
Discoverer of penicillin
Scottish, born Ayrshire (1881–1955)

21 ALAN TURING
Mathematician
English, born London (1912–54)

22 MICHAEL FARADAY
Scientist
English, born London (1791–1867)

23 OWAIN GLYNDWR
Leader of the Welsh, fought for independence in 1400
Welsh (died 1416)

24 HM QUEEN ELIZABETH II
Queen regnant 1952–
English, born London (1926–)

25 STEPHEN HAWKING
Theoretical physicist
English, born Oxford (1942–)

26 WILLIAM TYNDALE
Translator of the Bible
English, born Gloucestershire (1494–1536)

27 EMMELINE PANKHURST
Militant suffragette
English, born Manchester (1858–1928)

28 WILLIAM WILBERFORCE
Philanthropist and reformer
English, born Hull (1759–1833)

29 DAVID BOWIE
Singer, film and stage actor
English, born London (1947–)

30 GUY FAWKES
Conspirator
English, born York (1570–1606)

31 LEONARD CHESHIRE
War-hero and founder of Homes for the Disabled
English, born Cheshire (1917–92)

32 ERIC MORECAMBE
Comedian
English, born Morecambe Bay, Cumbria (1926–84)

33 DAVID BECKHAM
Footballer
English, born London (1975–)

34 THOMAS PAINE
Author
English, born Thetford, Norfolk (1737–1809)

35 BOUDICCA
Queen of Iceni; leader of revolt against Roman rule
English, born East Anglia (died AD62)

36 STEVE REDGRAVE
Oarsman and sports consultant
English, born Marlow, Berkshire (1962–)

37 THOMAS MORE
Lord Chancellor, scholar and author; canonized 1935
English, born London (1477–1535)

38 WILLIAM BLAKE
Visionary poet and painter
English, born London (1757–1827)

39 JOHN HARRISON
Horologist; discoverer of longitude
English, born Wakefield, Yorkshire (1693–1776)

40 HENRY VIII
King of England 1509–1547
English, born Greenwich (1491–1547)

41 CHARLES DICKENS
Novelist
English, born Portsmouth (1812–70)

42 FRANK WHITTLE
Aeronautical engineer and inventor
English, born Earlsdon, Coventry (1907–96)

43 JOHN PEEL
Radio and television presenter
English, born Heswall, near Liverpool (1939–)

44 JOHN LOGIE BAIRD
Television pioneer
Scottish, born Helensburgh (1888–1946)

45 ANEURIN BEVAN
Statesman; husband of Jennie Lee
Welsh, born Tredegar (1897–1960)

46 BOY GEORGE
Pop musician; member of Culture Club
English, born Kent (1961–)

46 DOUGLAS BADER
Pilot and Second World War hero
English, born London (1910–1982)

48 WILLIAM WALLACE
Patriot and hero of romance
Scottish, born Elderslie, Renfrewshire (1272?–1305)

49 FRANCIS DRAKE
Admiral and circumnavigator
English, born Tavistock, Devon (c.1541–1596)

be notorious

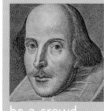

be a crowd pleaser

be inventive

be compassionate

be in tune

50 JOHN WESLEY
Methodist leader
English, born near Doncaster, Yorkshire (1703–91)

51 KING ARTHUR
King of Britons in medieval legend
Possibly born in Tintagel? (died 537)

52 FLORENCE NIGHTINGALE
Reformer of hospital nursing
English, born Florence, Italy (1820–1910)

53 T. E. LAWRENCE
'Lawrence of Arabia'; soldier and writer
Welsh, born Tremadoc, Carnarvonshire (1888–1935)

54 ROBERT FALCON SCOTT
Antarctic explorer
English, born Devon (1868–1912)

55 ENOCH POWELL
Politician and writer
English, born Birmingham (1912–98)

56 CLIFF RICHARD
Singer and actor
English, born Lucknow, India (1940–)

57 ALEXANDER GRAHAM BELL
Inventor
Scottish, born Edinburgh (1847–1922)

58 FREDDIE MERCURY
Vocalist; member of Queen
British Citizen, born Zanzibar (1946–91)

59 JULIE ANDREWS
Actress and singer
English, born Walton-on-Thames (1935–)

60 EDWARD ELGAR
Composer
English, born Broadheath, Worcestershire (1857–1934)

61 QUEEN ELIZABETH, THE QUEEN MOTHER
Wife of George VI
English, born London (1900–2002)

62 GEORGE HARRISON
Pop musician; member of The Beatles
English, born Liverpool (1943–2001)

63 DAVID ATTENBOROUGH
Naturalist and broadcaster
English, born London (1926–)

64 JAMES CONNOLLY
A leader of the 1916 Easter Rising
Irish, born Edinburgh (1868–1916)

65 GEORGE STEPHENSON
Inventor of the railway-engine
English, born Wylam, Northumberland (1781–1848)

66 CHARLIE CHAPLIN
Actor, director and producer
English, born London (1889–1977)

67 TONY BLAIR
Prime Minister 1997–
Scottish, born Edinburgh (1953–)

68 WILLIAM CAXTON
Inventor of the first printing press
English, born Weald of Kent (c.1422–91)

69 BOBBY MOORE
Footballer
English, born London (1941–93)

70 JANE AUSTEN
Novelist
English, born Steventon, Hampshire (1775–1817)

71 WILLIAM BOOTH
Founder of the Salvation Army
English, born Nottingham 1829–1912

72 HENRY V
King of England 1413–22
English, born Monmouth Castle, Wales (c.1387–22)

73 ALEISTER CROWLEY
Occult leader
English, born Leamington Spa (1875–1947)

74 ROBERT I 'THE BRUCE'
King of Scotland 1306–1329
Scottish, born Ayrshire (1274–1329)

75 BOB GELDOF
Musician
Irish, born Dublin (1954–)

76 THE UNKNOWN SOLDIER
Tomb in Westminster Abbey, London
Erected 1920

77 ROBBIE WILLIAMS
Pop singer
English, born Stoke-on-Trent, Staffordshire (1974–)

78 EDWARD JENNER
Physicist; discoverer of vaccination
English, born Berkeley (1749–1823)

79 DAVID LLOYD GEORGE
Prime Minister 1916–22
English, born Manchester (1858–1928)

80 CHARLES BABBAGE
Mathematician
English, born Devon (1791–1871)

81 GEOFFREY CHAUCER
Poet and author of *The Canterbury Tales* 1387–1400
English, born London (c.1340–1400)

82 RICHARD III
King of England 1483–85
English (1452–85)

83 J. K. ROWLING
Author
English, born Chipping Sodbury (1965–)

84 JAMES WATT
Engineer
Scottish, born Greenock (1736–1819)

85 RICHARD BRANSON
Business executive and entrepreneur
English, born Surrey (1950–)

86 BONO
Pop singer; member of U2
Irish, born Dublin (1960–)

87 JOHN LYDON
Musician; member of the Sex Pistols
English, born London (1956–)

88 MONTGOMERY OF ALAMEIN
Field-Marshal
English, born London (1887–1976)

89 DONALD CAMPBELL
Record-breaker
English, born Horley, Surrey (1921–67)

90 HENRY II
King of England 1154–1189
English, born Mans, Normandy (1133–89)

91 JAMES CLERK MAXWELL
Physicist
Scottish, born Edinburgh (1831–79)

92 J. R. R. TOLKIEN
Anglo-Saxon scholar and writer
English, born South Africa (1892–1973)

93 WALTER RALEGH
Soldier, sailor, poet and writer
English, born Devon (c.1552–1618)

94 EDWARD I
King of England 1272–1307
English, born Westminster (1239–1307)

95 BARNES WALLIS
Engineer and inventor
English, born Derbyshire (1887–1979)

96 RICHARD BURTON
Actor
Welsh, born Pontrhydyfen, South Wales (1925–84)

97 TONY BENN
Politician
English, born London (1925–)

98 DAVID LIVINGSTONE
Missionary and explorer
Scottish, born Blantyre (1813–73)

99 TIM BERNERS LEE
Director of the World Wide Web Consortium
English, born London (1955–)

100 MARIE STOPES
Palaeobotanist; pioneer and advocate of birth control
Scottish, born Edinburgh (1880–1958)

be a war hero

be better than men

believe in yourself

be brilliant

be prepared to die

One hundred heroes and more

MARK HARRISON

When the BBC invited the public to vote for their greatest Briton of all time, it wasn't only establishing the basis for an ingenious television series: it was also initiating an intriguing piece of opinion research. Coming at the start of a new millennium, the nominations made in the Great Britons poll invited a fascinating snapshot of what we most value and admire in the contribution made by others to our lives and the life of these Isles.

The huge response generated by the poll showed that the BBC had indeed pressed a button in the national psyche. Discussion of the poll began in the national press when it was first announced, and continued to resurface throughout the production period. Any mention of the series seemed to provoke enormously long and passionate conversations: was Isaac Newton greater than Charles Darwin; was Diana, Princess of Wales, worthy of nomination; would

the poll be won by a modern-day celebrity such as David Beckham or Geri Halliwell; where would Margaret Thatcher be placed? To ask people to name their greatest Briton, it seemed, was to invite them to throw open a window on all they abhor and all they hold dear.

Characters in context

Why? At a time when history is increasingly being taught as a confluence of social and economic contexts rather than as the deeds of great men, it might be expected that the very idea of voting for the greatest Briton would feel at best old-fashioned, and at worst irrelevant. But like most dichotomies, the supposed split between context and character is a false one. Characters are what give context meaning; context is what brings characters to life. It is doubtful that many who voted in the Great Britons poll seriously believe their chosen individuals singlehandedly altered the

An exhibition of celebrity photographs by Mario Testino attracted huge crowds to the National Portrait Gallery, London, in 2002. Yet the public have not voted any models, film stars or soap stars into the list of top 100 Great Britons.

course of history, or that their personalities were so flawlessly fine that they embodied everything admirable about our national identity. When describing someone as an all-time great, we are acknowledging that they have become an icon – and icons have a life and a meaning far beyond themselves. John Lennon would not have been remembered as great had it not been for his musical genius; but what then lifted him to the status of icon was the way he became representative, through his actions and beliefs as well as his music, of the life experience of a whole generation. Admiral Nelson was a deeply flawed and troubled man; yet his passion, daring and instinctive military brilliance remain both inspirational and achingly human. We know next to nothing about the life of William Shakespeare, yet his work remains inspirational to people all over the world. In short, every great character in history brings with them a rich context that helps us to understand ourselves – and that's why we attach to them so strongly.

In every life there are stories; and remarkable lives generate remarkable stories. It is through these stories that we gain a sense of how we fit into the world we have inherited. But the notion that history is essentially a treasure chest of stories is not to render it childish: it is to acknowledge that we all try to join the dots of where we come from through moments, myth and memory. Perhaps this is why history and biography have become increasingly popular forms of television programming: our awareness of the complexity of life is greater than ever, and we need an awful lot of stories, well told, to make sense of that.

What, then, are the stories suggested by the top 100 names in the Great Britons poll? There is an almost infinite number, of course; but a few particularly good ones stand out.

History matters more to us than celebrity
The clearest image to emerge through this snapshot of public opinion is that the British are sustained and stirred more by greatness forged in the white heat of history than by greatness conferred by the bright light of celebrity.

From (left) A. J. P. Taylor's first television lecture in 1957 to Simon Schama's *History of Britain* series in 2000, television has made history increasingly accessible, controversial and enjoyable to a mass audience.

Many people presumed that a poll such as this, taking place in the fame-drunk early 2000s, would resemble the index page of *Hello!* magazine. How wrong they were. Only twenty-two of the top 100 nominated Great Britons are alive today. There are no models, no film or soap stars, and only two living sports heroes: footballer David Beckham was ranked at no. 33, slightly ahead of Olympic rower Steve Redgrave at no. 36.

Significantly, the bulk of the living Britons come from the world of music – eleven in total (fourteen if broadened to include the DJ John Peel, and musical stars Michael Crawford and Julie Andrews). Some might see this as indeed the triumph of celebrity: how can pop stars be regarded as Great Britons? The answer, however, seems to lie precisely in the dominance of pop stars over any other representatives of popular culture. Most of us could chart the story of our lives through music. It is not by chance that *Desert Island Discs* endures, nor that the question 'What's your favourite music?' remains the most effective short-cut guide to personality. Our emotional identification with music is profound, and the pop-star nominations read like a pocket guide to post-war adolescence: Cliff Richard; John Lennon, Paul McCartney and George Harrison; David Bowie; Freddie Mercury; John Lydon; Boy George; Bob Geldof; Bono; Robbie Williams. It's a clutch of names that tells you as much about the life of modern Britain as a list of post-war prime ministers.

But despite the popularity of these musicians, we seem reluctant to award the mantle of greatness to those who might broadly be described as entertainers or crowd-pleasers. David Attenborough is the only TV presenter on the list; Richard Burton sits oddly with Julie Andrews and Michael Crawford in a threesome of the only actors; and in a nation famed for its sense of humour, Eric Morecambe and Charlie Chaplin are the only comedians remembered in this poll. There is no place for Peter Sellers or Spike Milligan; none for Richard Dimbleby or Alan Bennett; none for John Gielgud or Laurence Olivier. And none for Alfred Hitchcock.

White English males still rule history

The reason why history appears so dominated by white Englishmen is that we haven't had enough of it yet. Women's liberation, racism and Anglo-hegemony would not be the issues they are today if the nominations in this poll were more diverse. It is inevitable that history has most successfully recorded the efforts of those best placed to make a mark. Perhaps the clearest expression of this is the fact that while two white politicians renowned for their positions on race – William Wilberforce and Enoch Powell – finished high in the poll, there is not a single non-white face in

the top 100. Were this poll to be conducted again in a hundred years' time, it is unlikely this would be the case.

White and male though it undoubtedly is, the poll is not, however, quite as Anglocentric as it might at first appear. It's true that all the top ten are English, but a fifth of the nominations in the top 100 are from Ireland, Wales and Scotland – exactly the same as the proportion of the population of the British Isles that lives in these countries (not that residence is a precise guide to nationality).

Be born under a big sky

The geographical distribution of the top 100 Great Britons is reasonably even: you can be born anywhere and end up great. But if you want to end up being really great, it's best to start somewhere flat. Four of the top ten Great Britons were born in or around the fens: Nelson, at Burnham Thorpe on the Norfolk coast; Diana, also in Norfolk, at Sandringham; Isaac Newton at Woolsthorpe, near Grantham in Lincolnshire; and Oliver Cromwell at Huntingdon, Cambridgeshire.

These are not the only names from the east of England who feature prominently. Boudicca (at no. 35) was born in East Anglia, though we aren't sure exactly where; radical agitator Thomas Paine (no. 34) came from Thetford; and Paine's ideological opposite, Margaret Thatcher (no. 16) was born in Grantham.

How many of us born after 1945 didn't go through a time in our lives when we were devoted to at least one popular musician? From left to right: Cliff Richard by Derek Allen, 1958; Bob Geldof by John Swannell, 1989; Robbie Williams by Hamish Brown, 1998.

These two white politicians were concerned with issues of race in different ways, but there are no non-white faces in the top 100 nominations.

William Wilberforce (left) by Sir Thomas Lawrence, 1828, and Enoch Powell by Nick Sinclair, 1992.

Around a fifth of the top 100 were born in London, but none make it into the top ten, with the borderline exception of Elizabeth I, born in Greenwich. There does seem to be a rule, however, that the further one is born from London, the less the chance of being remembered as great. The great Scots in this poll were all born south of the Highlands, and all within striking distance of Glasgow and Edinburgh. The three Irish-born nominations, the Duke of Wellington (no. 15), and musicians Bob Geldof (no. 75) and Bono (no. 86), all come from Dublin. All the Welsh nominations were born near the English border except for the one many might mistakenly think was English – T. E. Lawrence or Lawrence of Arabia (no. 53), who was born in Tremadoc, Carnarvonshire. And only two nominations come from west of Wiltshire: King Arthur (no. 51), thought to be from Tintagel; and Francis Drake (no.49), from Tavistock.

The obvious explanation for the tailing off of great names in the further reaches of the British Isles is simply a decline in population density. But this only makes the prominence of names from around the Wash – an area so proverbially underpopulated that it is commonly mocked for its level of inbreeding – all the more intriguing.

We value our scientists more than our artists

Most startlingly absent from the top 100 are visual artists. Britain gave birth to John Constable, J. M.W. Turner, George Stubbs, Joshua Reynolds, Thomas Gainsborough, Francis Bacon, Henry Moore, David Hockney and Bridget Riley, to name only a few. Yet none have been honoured here. William Blake alone features in the top 100, though whether primarily for his painting or his poetry is unclear. Poetry is as much

Most of us learned the poetry of Keats at school but it appears that we have forgotten him as quickly as we forgot it. Similarly, John Constable features on the wall of more British homes than any other artist, so why doesn't he feature in the list? From left to right: John Keats by William Hilton, after Joseph Severn, c.1822; John Constable, self-portrait, c.1799–1804; *The Hay Wain* by John Constable, 1821.

neglected in this poll as painting: Keats, Yeats, Burns, Wordsworth, Shelley, Byron, Betjeman and Hughes are all notable for their absence.

But if there appears to be a collective amnesia when it comes to aesthetics, there's something approaching total recall when it comes to those who displayed scientific and technical ingenuity. One-fifth of all the top 100 nominations are for names from the world of science, engineering and invention, from William Caxton (the printing press) to Tim Berners Lee (the World Wide Web); from Edward Jenner (pioneer of vaccination) to Barnes Wallis (inventor of the bouncing bomb). The presence in the top ten of Charles Darwin and Isaac Newton – two names that would surely get automatic selection in any team sheet of British Greats – is unsurprising. It is the presence of Isambard Kingdom Brunel that reveals our deep respect for those who harnessed science. Relatively little has been written or said about Brunel in recent years, but he has remained the symbol of an entrepreneurial spirit in engineering that many think of as distinctively British, yet distinctly lacking in Britain today.

Building ideas and building bridges

The recognition we give to science and technology at the expense of the arts doesn't make us a nation of complete trainspotters, however. Those who led social movements and reform campaigns, who did charitable work and who built our legal and democratic structures are also well remembered. Leonard Cheshire and Florence Nightingale finished higher in the poll than George Stephenson and James Watt. Some might argue that Lloyd George, Aneurin Bevan and Emmeline Pankhurst deserved even higher places in the pecking order of greatness than nos 79, 45 and 27 respectively. But it might surprise others to find Alfred the Great (educational reformer as well as monarch) and Thomas Paine (radical political agitator) appearing as high as nos 14 and 34.

The rise and fall of kings and queens

If you wanted to choose a single job description most likely to secure you a place in the public's lasting affections, it would still have to be member of a royal family. No fewer than fourteen royals (including Boudicca and Robert Bruce) make the Great Britons list. And yet the list still makes better reading for republicans than royalists. The present royal family makes only a muted appearance, with Queen Elizabeth II at no. 24 and the Queen Mother at no. 61 (although had the poll taken place after the latter's death, she would most probably have been placed higher). It is Princess Diana, the individual generally credited with changing perceptions of the modern royal family, who makes it into the top ten. Admittedly she is joined there by Elizabeth I, the quintessential monarch, but also nearby is Oliver Cromwell, the quintessential republican.

The Tudor Galleries are some of the most visited rooms in the National Portrait Gallery, London. Their popularity with older visitors and school groups alike reflects the broad public interest in the history of the British monarchy.

Everyone loves a soldier

Traditionally we build monuments to our war heroes above all others, and the Great Britons poll is another such monument. Winston Churchill's prominent position surely has more to do with his leadership in war than his achievements in peacetime. War calls for daring, for leadership and for fine words, all of which we can't help but admire. War seems to appeal to our primitive instinct to idolise anyone prepared to fight for us, protect us and to advance our cause. Nelson is perhaps the ultimate war hero, since he died in action. Wellington, Robert Bruce, Owain Glyndwr, Henry V, Lawrence of Arabia and Field-Marshal Montgomery are among the other fighting men remembered here. Many voters also chose to mark the contribution of the thousands of ordinary men and women who have fallen in our defence by nominating the Unknown Soldier.

The Great Britons poll does nothing to contradict the observation made by one of its top ten members, William Shakespeare, more than four hundred years ago, that some are born to greatness, some achieve greatness, and some have greatness thrust upon them. But is it possible to speak of any characteristic common to all those who have earned the epithet of great?

One thing all the top ten people in the Great Britons poll certainly have in common is that they wouldn't have been much fun to live with. Between them they display the full range of human flaws: depression, disloyalty, dishonesty, selfishness, vanity and cruelty. Even Darwin, a quiet, faithful family man, was so stressed by the burden of his ideas that he was almost permanently ill. In honouring him, we remember a man who gave us a revolutionary new understanding of the origin and development of the human species. His wife Emma's experience of him, on the other hand, was of a man who required almost constant nursing and who suffered from incessant nausea and flatulence. Behind the top 100 Great Britons, there are at least a hundred further forgotten heroes like her.

Looking at the personalities that feature strongly in this poll it would seem there may be one single unifying motto: 'Be great at all costs; history will forgive you.'

Essay illustrations are listed on page 169.

Why biography matters to us

BRIAN HARRISON

We all enjoy listing things in rank order. A sense of power comes with compiling lists that make the world seem tidier than it really is, and by weighing one Great Briton against another we get all the boost to the morale that comes with playing God. We raise this one up, scale that one down, and take it upon ourselves to judge people who have ascended way beyond our sphere. And because we no longer regard the great as a different species, we have all the fascination of probing into precisely how it was that they came to make (or came to appear to make) such a major impact on their times. What strange chance, what quirk of personality, what unusual combination of experiences enabled them to rise so far above us? What precise circumstances prompted that creative moment when the great musical or literary composition took place, the major scientific break through, the brilliant strategic move, the daring political initiative? From listing and ranking we get all the enjoyment that comes from feeling that we've at last got a grip on wide sweeps of history. And there is a purely recreational element: here we have an up-market version of the Derby and the Grand National. Without their much-publicised short-listings, for example, who would feel the slightest interest in who gets the Booker Prize for literature or the Mercury Music Prize?

Meritocracy

There's nothing new, of course, about putting people into rank order. In aristocratic societies where rank is decided by birth, inheritance and precedent, there's no place for selection by examination, but the increasing complexity of nineteenth-century society forced the Victorians to invent the public examination as a way of identifying and encouraging talent. During the twentieth century we came to take meritocratic appointment to public positions for granted. So long as people have got the talent or motivation, they now earn their position through ingenuity, enterprise, effort and perception of opportunity. An early example of meritocratic honours is the award of the Victoria Cross for bravery. When 100 VCs from all ranks joined together at the inauguration of the Unknown Soldier's tomb on 11 November 1920, the *Manchester Guardian* appropriately described them as 'a little democracy of valour'. In most situations, however, the qualities worth rewarding are less obvious, and in a socially mobile community where mutual assessment is continuous, we need league tables for the same reason that we need headhunters: no longer is there in Britain a closed, mutually acquainted, face-to-face elite whose membership and values are widely acknowledged and accepted. In an increasingly busy and specialised world, we feel the need for reach-me-down statistical guidance in finding our bearings.

The people's vote

The taste for rank-ordering flows not only from meritocracy but also from democracy, with all its egalitarian connotations. The other ranks subject their officers to scrutiny – when casting votes at elections, answering opinion-polls, ranking television programmes or filling in questionnaires. To rank Great Britons, alive or dead, is a sort of democratised honours list that covers the whole of British history, bringing with it the risk that the importance of well-known contemporaries will be inflated by comparison with tried-and-tested figures from the past. Nowadays we even feel we should have a role in compiling the official honours list. Its publication was once awaited

A crowded day for the Beatles

Exit the Beatles, and fans break through to chase the group's Rolls

Screaming fans wait outside the Palace

Fans go wild as M.B.E. boys drop in at the Palace

By KEITH GRAVES

THE QUEEN held an investiture at Buckingham Palace yesterday. She was graciously pleased to confer the honour of Member of the Most Excellent Order of the British Empire on John Lennon Esq., Richard Starkey Esq., George Harrison Esq., and Paul McCartney Esq.

From Liverpool Sound to Establishment Image — Paul, George, John, and Ringo with their M.B.E.s

Since the award of MBEs to The Beatles in 1965, the Queen's Birthday honours list has generated publicity by endorsing celebrities alongside public service workers. Yet ranking Great Britons, alive or dead, brings with it the risk that the importance of contemporary celebrities will be inflated by comparison with historical figures.

with bated breath by people keen to discover whom the establishment had endorsed; yet now the general public participate indirectly, and even directly, in compiling it. They participate indirectly because a smaller proportion of the higher honours reward public service, and a larger proportion retrospectively endorse activities that have already received popular endorsement – whether through wealth, fame or popularity. So sporting and media personalities abound in the New Year and Queen's Birthday honours lists. The precedents were set when knighthoods went to Stanley Matthews in 1965 and Alf Ramsey in 1967, and when The Beatles got their MBEs in 1965. Lower down in the honours list, John Major's reforms made public participation in the ranking process more direct, with opportunities for the public to suggest names, often of voluntary workers. Seventy of the 970 honours announced on 31 December 1993 had emerged from the new system of nominations by the public; a further 130 of those then honoured had been nominated by the public, though they had already been under consideration by Downing Street.

On that occasion the government received 10,000 nomination forms from the public, covering 7,500 people. Under Tony Blair, people could even volunteer themselves for selection as 'people's peers', the first fifteen of whom were announced in April 2001.

League tables

Rank-ordering also flows from the consumerism that accompanies democracy. League tables are spreading through all areas of British life. The Top Twenty charts of gramophone record favourites began in the 1950s; lists of record-breakers were first published in the *Guinness Book of Records* in 1955; and service-providers are now ranked in such books as the *Good Food Guide* (since 1951) and the *Good Hotel Guide* (since 1977). From the 1990s there was an increasing fashion for league tables as a quick and open way of deciding how public funds should be assigned and how good were the services that public bodies provided to clients who were increasingly viewed as customers. Hence the much-publicised national league tables for welfare services, hospitals, local authorities, schools and universities.

It's worth discussing whether we should be ranking Great Britons in a single list. Such a wealth of biographical information has now been collected by institutions like the National Portrait Gallery and the *Dictionary of National Biography* that we could easily, and perhaps more usefully, compile separate league tables under different headings – enterprise, talent, intellect, wealth, courage, notoriety, popularity, power, impact, originality – all running in parallel. We could then apply our desired weighting for different types of desired quality, and mathematically conflate the tables into a single and overall rank order, which would be less random than a single table impressionistically compiled. It is also wrong to assume that there is any objective measure of 'greatness'. The traits that society values change over time. Holiness would still rank high today among the qualities valued by the minority who go to church, but their numbers have long been in decline; we are nowadays primarily concerned with assessing achievement in this world rather than with aspirations for the next. Again, we now seem to know so much about politics – illuminated as the politician's world is by instant biography,

investigative journalism, political science and media manipulation – that politicians, too, have fallen from their pedestals. The politicians' critics, on the other hand – media people, reformers, pressure-group leaders, 'freedom fighters' – are much more likely to receive obituaries in the national press than was once the case. And in an increasingly settled, prosperous society, whose armed services depend increasingly on technological prowess, the valuation of physical courage in war is less all-pervasive than it once was. The decline of empire, the horrors of two world wars, and the illumination of war's shocking realities by the modern media push other qualities up the charts: creativity, spontaneity, originality and sporting prowess, for example. Entertainers, performers and games players all gain from this, not just in the charts but also in the honours lists.

Hero-worship

But the main attraction of ranking Great Britons has yet to be mentioned: the sheer fascination of the subject matter. Biographies fascinate us for several reasons. This is partly because self-discovery is nowadays a major reason for reading biography. The modern media tear away the privacy that once lent mystique to those in authority, and we feel qualified to judge them less reverently. Indeed, we quite readily imagine ourselves into their shoes: but for accidents of birth or opportunity, we tell ourselves, we too could have been there. It was not always so. Nations once put their heroes in pantheons; the streets of their capital cities abounded in heroes commemorated with statues on plinths and pillars, and by street names; they even, in the case of the French nineteenth-century Positivists, erected a pseudo-religion around the hero figure. The subjects of biography – aristocrats, war heroes, film stars, scientific geniuses – once widely supposed to belong to a different species, we now treat with something approaching familiarity. Modern British biography has let in daylight upon magic, which was something that Walter Bagehot, that shrewd nineteenth-century analyst of British monarchy, always knew would undermine authority.

The British enjoy listing things in rank order, illustrated by the popularity of awards such as the Booker Prize for literature, the Turner Prize for art and the Mercury Prize for music. Whilst bookmakers accept bets on the winners, these awards also help to influence public opinion. Sales of Talvin Singh's album *OK* rose considerably after he won the Mercury Prize in 1999.

Modern biographers have become less keen on hero-figures, and more interested in exploring the darker elements of human behaviour and motivation. Here the politician Oswald Mosley (1896–1980) is seen addressing a meeting of British fascists at Victoria Park Square in the East End of London on 14 October 1936.

So whereas escapism was once a prime attraction of biography, self-knowledge has become more important. Not self-improvement, though. The Victorians saw biography as offering guidance on how to 'improve' oneself in manners, speech and education. The Liberal philosopher John Stuart Mill recalled in his autobiography of 1873 that his father 'was fond of putting into my hands books which exhibited men of energy and resource in unusual circumstances, struggling against difficulties and overcoming them'. Much nineteenth-century biography and autobiography aimed to encourage the latent entrepreneur into life, to advertise the attractions of educational and cultural self-cultivation, and to urge forward the intelligent or the able person who was trapped within a class below his deserts. Readers of modern biography, however, are less eager for hero figures; they are keener to locate themselves in relation to the subject and to gain entertainment, without necessarily wishing to move up socially or culturally.

Anti-heroism

Several long-term twentieth-century trends have been at work here. It looked at one time as though nineteenth-century secularised liberalism would place human self-direction at the centre of things by overcoming tradition, superstition and notions of divine predestination. In the twentieth century, however, Freudian psychology and Marxism undermined nineteenth-century rationalism and liberalism from two directions, and their erosion of faith in the individual's autonomy was reinforced by inter-war Bloomsbury's anti-Victorian 'debunking' biographical fashion. Then, after 1939, the awful consequences of fascist hero-worship carried the reaction against hero figures still further. Whereas nineteenth-century Britain was much preoccupied with warding off threats to the authority of government, the emphasis after the Second World War shifted to containing government: to defending civil liberties, drafting bills and declarations of universal rights, and erecting tribunals and procedures that would protect all citizens against the abuse of power. Several twentieth-century climacterics edged us further along this route: for example, the deceptions in British policy that lay behind the Suez crisis in 1956, the attempts at cover-up by President Nixon in the United States during the early 1970s, and the disastrous inefficiencies and inhumanities that governmental secrecy nourished within the USSR, not to mention President Clinton's prevarication in the 1990s when trying to conceal his activities within the Oval Office.

The road to individuality

There is a second and related reason for biography's continued popularity: its subject matter has opened out so as to become more interesting. For biography to exist at all, the individual must be valued for his own sake and should not be cramped into a stereotype. Biography can arise only when value is attached to what makes a person unique, and this did not come quickly. As recently as the nineteenth century, most people were assigned predictable social roles and status and were expected to identify with the standard models that were associated with gender, social class, nationality, religion, and so on. In British biography, markers along the long road to individuality have been James Boswell's *Life of Samuel Johnson* (1791), J. A. Froude's biography of the historian Thomas Carlyle (1882–4), E. S. Purcell's *Cardinal Manning* (1895),

James Boswell's *Life of Samuel Johnson* (1791) was arguably the first British biography. It also demonstrates the power of the medium to secure enduring celebrity for its subjects.
Samuel Johnson by James Barry, c. 1778–80.

Edmund Gosse's *Father and Son* (1907) and Lytton Strachey's *Eminent Victorians* (1918).

Privacy in retreat

Associated with this process has been the biographer's willingness to discuss ever more personal dimensions of the individual's life. A tactful piety has been ousted by the pressure for transparency. In his biography of J. M. Keynes, Roy Harrod could, as recently as 1951, feel the urge to 'pause at the threshold and not seek to pry among the inner eddies of his subject's emotions', claiming that 'the secrets of the heart must remain secret'. All that came to an end with Michael Holroyd's *Life of Lytton Strachey* (1967–8), and no holds were henceforth barred. Keynes's more recent biographer Robert Skidelsky, discussing Harrod's *Keynes*, points out that, for Harrod, 'truth, in the sense of fidelity to the facts, was subordinate to uplift'. Behind all this lies modern British society's retreat from reticence and modesty; our valuation of privacy is now only selective. Privacy against intrusive authority preoccupies us at least as much as ever, but during the late twentieth century we became far less coy about keeping confidences. With the publication of political diaries from the 1970s onwards – by Richard Crossman, Barbara Castle, Tony Benn, Woodrow Wyatt and Alan Clark – conversations once private were exposed for all to hear. Furthermore, fewer of us are now content with the idea that virtue is its own reward. There were Victorian working people who thought that even the attempt to photograph them constituted a form of violation or theft, and for people higher up (especially women), it was for centuries the essence of good breeding to remain out of the public limelight, or to appear in public only on special occasions. Nowadays, by contrast, the eagerness of some people for their fifteen minutes of fame is so great that they are prepared to tell all in their bid for the sixteenth minute, aiming with little scruple to advance their confected careers. The colour supplement and the chat show have become an arena for people who seem to be 'personalities' or 'celebrities' and nothing else. People, as well as commodities, are now required to sell themselves.

Broader scope

So far I have been talking about the healthy appetite of the general reader for biography, but there has also been a shift towards biography among professional historians, nourished by the disillusion that some of them feel with the contextual and sociological approaches to history that were fashionable in the 1960s and 1970s. Too often the ambitiously quantitative and comprehensive analyses that had been lavishly funded ended by delivering heaped-up figures that reflected only their compilers' preconceptions, or even by delivering nothing at all. Unlike the biographer's relatively straightforward, individualistic and inexpensive techniques, the pseudo-scientific complexity and self-conscious teamwork of the historian-as-social-scientist may have brought academic prestige, but it was the biographer who arguably gave better value for time and effort expended. Nor did the subsequent post modern countervailing anti-biographical trend, flowing from the academic study of literature, significantly effect historians, who have always thought context all-important when studying a text.

Biography, then, has for some time been growing more democratic and open in its approach. A further attraction is that it has become less exclusive in its subject matter. Well-bred Victorian women remained in the private sphere, leaving the public sphere to fathers, husbands and sons. 'No statistics are needed to prove that the woman's opportunities of distinction were infinitesimal in the past, and are very small compared with men's,' wrote Sidney Lee, the second editor of the *Dictionary of National Biography* (*DNB*), in 1896. As recently as 1929, Virginia Woolf – daughter of Leslie Stephen, the *DNB*'s first editor – wrote of women that 'anonymity runs in their blood'; she claimed that their literary achievement could not compare with that of men because 'the desire to be veiled still possesses them'. So she crusaded biographically on behalf of the lesser-known. 'Since so much is known that used to be unknown,' she wrote in 1939, 'the question now inevitably asks itself, whether the lives of great men only should be recorded. Is not

As the daughter of the first editor of the *Dictionary of National Biography* and a writer herself, Virginia Woolf argued for the inclusion of more women in this monumental reference work. Virginia Woolf by George Charles Beresford, 1902.

anyone who has lived a life, and left a record of that life, worthy of biography – the failures as well as the successes, the humble as well as the illustrious? And what is greatness? And what smallness?' The biographer, she went on, 'must revise our standards of merit and set up new heroes for our admiration'. The attitudes of her father and his successor helped to ensure that only four per cent of the articles in the *DNB* concerned women. The balance of the *DNB*'s coverage of centuries earlier than our own will probably always be skewed heavily towards men, if only because evidence on the 'women's sphere' is relatively scarce. None the less, the *DNB* is now being completely revised and enlarged for publication on-line and in book form in 2004, and a tenth of its articles will be devoted to women. This shift has been secured largely by looking for the women who were always

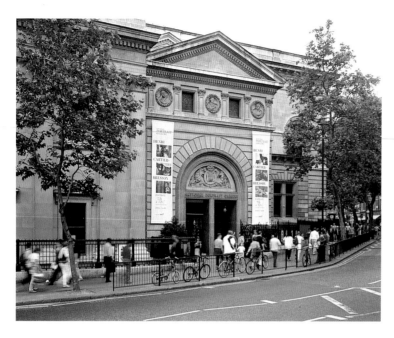

In recent years new displays at the National Portrait Galleries in London (left) and Edinburgh, and research for the *New Dictionary of National Biography* (above), have helped to raise awareness of the contribution of a broader range of individuals to British society.

there. If, for example, you include more articles drawn from occupations such as social work, charity, religious activity and teaching, you find more women who deserve inclusion, even from among those who fully accepted contemporary separate-sphere notions of their role.

Every life is interesting

Woolf's plea for a wider range of biographical subjects ran in parallel with E. M. Forster's liberal-minded belief that hero-worship is 'a dangerous vice'. For him, one of democracy's minor merits is that 'it does not . . . produce that unmanageable type of citizen known as the Great Man', but 'produces instead different kinds of small men – a much finer achievement'. The twentieth century has nourished the democratic notion that everyone is in some sense interesting, and in the 1960s acted upon that belief in the movement for 'oral history', which set out to interview 'ordinary' people on a wide scale. 'In order to write one's reminiscences it is not at all necessary to be a great man . . .', the Russian political thinker Alexander Herzen had written many years earlier, adding, 'It is quite enough to be simply a human being, to have something to

tell, and not merely to desire to tell it but at least have some little ability to do so. Every life is interesting; if not the personality, then the environment, the country are interesting, the life itself is interesting.'

There is one further incentive to reading and writing biography in the United Kingdom: the need to discover our collective bearings. We feel the need, in a rapidly changing society within a country whose international standing is shifting, to discover quite what sort of people we are. Changing relationships between the constituent parts of the United Kingdom, and the advent of immigrants from all parts of the world, force us to reappraise our national identity. Biography is not of course the only way to do this: we can conduct national debates on devolution, investigate the origins of the union, conduct opinion surveys and watch television programmes on 'the making of the nation'. Hence the popularity of books like Linda Colley's *Britons: Forging the Nation 1707–1837* (1992) and of television series like Simon Schama's *History of Britain*. But biography and portraiture are also important to national self-discovery, as a brief concluding account of three Victorian institutions will show. First, there was the scheme to identify the homes of famous people. The idea of putting plaques on buildings once occupied by famous people began with a scheme launched in London by the Royal Society of Arts in 1867, the year in which it put up its plaque to commemorate Byron, and by 1901 the Society had put up thirty-six plaques. The scheme was taken over by the London County Council in that year, and there are now nearly seven hundred, with similar schemes in other cities.

Instruction by image

The link with national self-discovery was also present from the outset in a second Victorian institution: the National Portrait Gallery. When Lord Stanhope was urging its creation in the House of Lords on 4 March 1856, he cited in support a letter from the historian Thomas Carlyle, to whose imagination portraiture was a stimulus. 'Often have I found a portrait superior in real instruction to half-a-dozen written biographies...', Carlyle wrote, continuing, 'I have found that the portrait was as a small lighted candle by which the biographies could for the first time be read, and some human interpretation be made of them.' The need to educate artists in aesthetic technique and historical accuracy, and the need to enlighten the general public on the nation's history were prominent among the arguments for such a gallery in the debate of 1856; its portraits, said Stanhope, 'would be useful as an incitement to honourable exertion'. The Gallery was set up, and the archaeologist and politician A. H. Layard claimed in 1888 that 'an attentive walk' through it 'is a useful lesson, easily and pleasantly learnt, in the history of England in its various branches ... We know of no place where parents can take their children with greater profit.'

The National Portrait Gallery's links with the third Victorian institution, the *Dictionary of National Biography*, were present from the *DNB*'s earliest years; Leslie Stephen, the *DNB*'s first editor, was a trustee of the Gallery; there were many informal links between the two bodies; and the *DNB* carefully listed portraits of its subjects at the end of each memoir. The founding editor of the *New DNB* to be published in 2004, Colin Matthew, was also a trustee of the Gallery, and he was keen from the start that the Gallery should advise the *DNB* on portraiture. With the help of a project run by the Gallery's nineteenth-century curator Peter Funnell, the *New DNB* will allocate a likeness to 10,000 of its 50,000 subjects. A real effort has been made to get illustrations for the *New DNB*'s growth areas: business people, for example, and women. Both the *DNB*'s and the Gallery's criteria for inclusion are in one important respect similar: selection is non-partisan and comprehensive, and villains as well as saints get in. Since 1969, however, one further similarity – the exclusion of the living – has been removed: the Gallery, dependent on portraits, was less confident than the *DNB* that people would leave an appropriate record behind.

The national myth

It is perhaps through the route of national self-discovery that the idea of 'greatness', dismissed earlier at the front door, re-enters the national stage by the back entrance. For however much we may depreciate the distinctive contribution of Queen Elizabeth I or Winston Churchill to the history of Britain during their lifetimes, their contribution to the national self-image can hardly be denied. Nor are we alone among nations in placing the great at the centre of our national myth. If Lloyd George and Winston Churchill epitomise national resistance to Germany in two world wars, Joan of Arc and General de Gaulle are central to the French national self-image, F. D. Roosevelt is central to the story of America's inter-war economic recovery, and Nelson Mandela is central to South Africa's new-found racial harmony. Nor is it only the respectable who play such roles in national consciousness, as Ned Kelly, Australia's latter-day Robin Hood, reminds us. So at the outset of the twenty-first century, however meritocratic, democratic and debunking our mood may be, we still feel a need for Great Britons.

The top ten Britons

JOHN COOPER

Elizabeth I

William Shakespeare

Oliver Cromwell

Isaac Newton

Horatio Nelson

Why do some people find lasting fame for their actions, while others lapse into obscurity?

What makes an individual truly 'great'?

The following chapters discuss the lives of the top ten British men and women voted for in the Great Britons poll. Organised in chronological order, each chapter is introduced by one of the BBC documentary presenters, who makes a personal and passionate case for the greatness of their subject.

The main text explores and celebrates the iconography of each of the top ten, examining the interplay of image and reputation both during their lifetime and posthumously. A key aspect of that interplay is the dynamic of its creation: to what extent did the Great Britons themselves contribute to it, and how far was it the work of others?

William Shakespeare's image was largely constructed posthumously, his immortalisation confirmed in a mass of derivative paintings, prints and sculptures. Isambard Kingdom Brunel's entire life was consumed by his engineering projects; he sought no other reflection of his achievements. Charles Darwin, an unwilling celebrity, was patient with the demands of photographers and artists, and relied on others to defend his theories publicly. John Lennon's initial image as an aggressive rocker may have been his own creation, but later transformations were strongly influenced by discerning women.

Oliver Cromwell and Elizabeth I knew the importance of visual representation in confirming and defining the nature of their authority. Colourful and flattering portraits of the Queen survive, certainly, but evidence suggests that much of the content was the work of courtiers and ministers, while recent interpretations suggest that Cromwell's 'warts and all' attitude was as much political as personal.

Isaac Newton had a robust approach to self-promotion, commissioning and donating dozens of portraits. Posterity produced images glorifying him, from patron saint of the Enlightenment to guiding spirit of the British Library. Horatio Nelson set out the agenda for his own immortality, briefing his biographers, and anticipating his own death scene in conversations with artists. Winston Churchill, too, had a sense of personal destiny, but unlike Nelson, survived his defining moments to relive them in a published narrative of his own devising, and to fight a last battle for his personal image.

Diana, Princess of Wales, found herself a celebrity, subject because of her beauty and status to the insatiable demands of the media. She learned to turn this to her own advantage, and in so doing defined her image for posterity.

These chapters demonstrate that the majority of the nation's favourite Britons were conscious of their place in public culture, even if they allowed others to contribute to their image. The illustrations may help to make tangible their attitudes, attributes and occasionally their failings, but it is a testimony to each Briton's achievement that their portraits remain such a dynamic part of the nation's self-image.

Isambard Kingdom Brunel

Charles Darwin

Winston Churchill

John Lennon

Diana, Princess of Wales

Elizabeth I

Queen Elizabeth I was an expert in the substance and performance of monarchy. Her defiance of Catholic Spain consolidated England as a Protestant nation state

'She combined extraordinary political gifts and intelligence with femininity and magnanimity'

Michael Portillo, politician

Queen Elizabeth I of England was the only monarch voted by the public into the top ten for the BBC *Great Britons* series. She has long been a favourite of the school syllabus, and she's popular not least as a role model for women. She has been kept in the public eye recently through the television series *Elizabeth I*, presented by David Starkey; through the film *Elizabeth*, starring Cate Blanchett; and through an Oscar-winning portrayal by Dame Judi Dench in *Shakespeare in Love*.

Partly because she has been 'done' so much, it wasn't easy to decide how to provide a new angle on her, and even though she made it easily into the top ten, I could see problems in convincing people that she is the greatest Briton of all. Part of the problem is that we relate to Elizabeth through her portraits. They are magnificent, but they are not approachable. They were painted as propaganda, designed to show her as powerful, self-assured and, of course, beautiful. Their symbolism and their formality are impenetrable for a modern lay audience.

Another difficulty is that the present day is always so condescending towards the past. Rather like teenagers who think themselves the first generation to discover sex, we tend to regard people in the past as less complex or subtle than ourselves, or we arrogantly give importance to things in their lives only if they seem 'relevant' to what has happened since. Maybe we are a bit less patronising towards more recent historic figures whom we can see in newsreels. I was afraid that Elizabeth, being 469 years old, would be at a disadvantage in this television election.

As a politician I couldn't help being on the look-out for the qualities that enabled Elizabeth to gain, keep and use power. As I read about her, I was often sent reeling by the evidence of how sophisticated an operator she was. I hope I will be forgiven for my banality, since many modern parallels swam into my head and, I confess, found their way into my film.

To understand what I mean, start by thinking about those portraits. They show a fixation with 'image' in its literal sense. Only reproductions of official portraits were allowed to be sold to the public. The sixteenth-century spin doctors presented her as eternally youthful. They made a cult out of her virginity, which they presented as the ultimate self-sacrifice by a monarch married to England and mother to all her citizens. The image was designed to invite the people of England to worship their Queen, to worship the virgin. Even Peter Mandelson never attempted such an ambitious manipulation of public opinion!

Elizabeth succeeded Bloody Mary (Mary I, 1516–58), whose reign was a disaster: a half-foreign Queen, married to a foreigner, who burned three hundred people at the stake in her attempt to re-introduce Catholicism, and lost Calais to France for good measure. As Elizabeth ascended the throne, the message from her Hatfield headquarters was 'New Queen, new start' and 'Things can only get better'.

The Queen's progresses around her kingdom showed off her thousands of dresses. She plunged herself into the crowds, who found her extraordinarily approachable. No one who met her ever forgot the moment of doing so, and after her death her memory acquired the status of a myth. (How easily and fittingly those words could also have been written for Diana, Princess of Wales.)

Elizabeth was a superb rhetorician. Her speech at Tilbury in 1588, to a ramshackle army expecting a Spanish invasion, was a brilliant and original appeal to the English underdog repelling the foreign bully. I believe it has set the standard for great patriotic speeches ever since. It pre-dated Shakespeare's speech for Henry V at Agincourt, and its traces persist in the wartime speeches of Winston Churchill (1874–1965).

I have seen at first hand how hard it is for a leader to resist a determined establishment that thinks it knows best.

Elizabeth I 1533–1603

7 September 1533	Henry VIII's second wife, Anne Boleyn (1501–36), gives birth to Protestant daughter Elizabeth at Greenwich Palace, London
1536	Anne Boleyn is beheaded for adultery and treason
1547	Henry VIII (1491–1547) dies and is succeeded in turn by his youngest child, Edward VI (1537–53) and eldest daughter, Mary I (1516–58)
1553	As a Catholic, Mary I feels threatened by the Protestant Elizabeth and imprisons her in the Tower of London for two months
November 1558	Elizabeth becomes Queen
1559	Protestantism is re-established in England through the Acts of Supremacy and Uniformity
1568	Mary, Queen of Scots (1542–87) is taken into custody when she arrives in England from Scotland
1572	Elizabeth sends army to aid the French Huguenots following a massacre in France in which over 3,000 Huguenots were killed
1577	Francis Drake sets out in the *Golden Hind* to circumnavigate the globe, returning triumphantly in 1580
8 February 1587	Mary, Queen of Scots is executed after being found guilty of plotting against Elizabeth
1588	The Spanish invasion force, the Armada, is destroyed
1594	The Nine Years War starts, in which hundreds of English troops are killed
24 March 1603	Elizabeth I dies, aged 69, and is succeeded by James I (1566–1625), son of Mary, Queen of Scots

For forty-five years Elizabeth saw off a male establishment that thought she should marry, or at the very least name an heir. Those men underestimated her. She resisted them subtly and effectively. She used every trick in the book: she agreed, flattered, changed her mind, and lost her temper. It was an extraordinary display of iron will by a woman in a man's world determined to get her way. As I read about how she defied them for forty-five years, I couldn't hold back my vivid recollections of Margaret Thatcher in power.

However, it's also the sides of Elizabeth that she carefully excluded from the portraits that I hope will win her extra votes. The Queen wasn't Superwoman. She was filled with human frailties. She had frequent attacks of nerves. She went completely soppy when in love. And she was nearly destroyed by scandal over her relationship with Robert Dudley (1532?–1588).

By the standards of the day Elizabeth was an extremely merciful monarch. I believe her imprisonment in the Tower of London at the age of twenty-one may have strengthened her natural tendency to compassion. The Queen agonised over death warrants, even when the victims were highly dangerous to her. She loathed religious bigotry and she created an English middle way: Protestantism with Roman tinges, bells and candles.

Her tolerance and sense of fun led her to resist the Puritans, for example over their attempts to close the London theatres. I believe she created the conditions for an English renaissance that included William Shakespeare (1564–1616) and Christopher Marlowe (1564–93) among its writers, and William Byrd (1543–1623) and Thomas Tallis (c.1505–85) among its musicians. I would go further in my argument, and trace back to Elizabeth the origins of that British tolerance and diversity on which we pride ourselves today. While we are talking of her legacy, it's worth remembering that she gave encouragement and honours to Sir Walter Ralegh (1552–1618), who founded the colony of Virginia in her name, taking the English language to the New World for the first time.

In dangerous times, Elizabeth I calmed the religious storms dividing England, kept us out of most foreign wars, and survived to die of old age. She combined extraordinary political gifts and intelligence with femininity and magnanimity. Any one of her qualities could carry the stamp of greatness, but they were all combined in this one great Briton, this one exceptional woman.

The image of a queen

'I know I have the body of a weak and feeble woman, but I have the heart and stomach of a king, and of a king of England too.'

Speech to the troops at Tilbury on the approach of the Armada, 1588, in Lord Somers, *A Third Collection of Scarce and Valuable Tracts* (1751) p.196

Elizabeth I
Unknown artist, c.1575
Oil on panel, 1130 × 787mm (44½ × 31")
National Portrait Gallery, London (NPG 2082)

OPPOSITE
Elizabeth I known as The Rainbow Portrait
Attributed to Marcus Gheeraerts the Younger c.1600
Oil on canvas, 1270 × 1016mm (50½ × 40")
Hatfield House, Hertfordshire

The Rainbow Portrait is a complex pictorial puzzle. *NON SINE SOLE IRIS* says the Latin inscription; 'no rainbow (*iris*) without the sun (*sole*)'. Elizabeth I, the sun, brings the rainbow of peace. On her left sleeve the serpent of her wisdom holds a heart in its mouth, symbolising a mastery over passions suitable for a great ruler. The eyes and ears on her dress indicate her all-seeing, all-hearing omniscience. Her face is youthful to stress her enduring vigour.

The National Portrait Gallery is fortunate in possessing a full-length portrait of Elizabeth I, the last of the Tudors, which is elaborate, mysterious and cryptic in its symbolism, yet blazingly clear as a statement of authority (p.35). Hanging nearby is another portrait of Elizabeth, painted a little less than twenty years earlier, which presents an image of great dignity in a plain and straightforward way (left). What happened to bring about such a change of image in that interval?

As the unmarried, Protestant, female monarch of a small island kingdom, Elizabeth was as vulnerable as the country she ruled in the Europe of the early 1580s. She was by now beyond marriageable age, so could no longer use negotiations for her hand as a bargaining counter in international affairs. She had finally been excommunicated by the Pope and abandoned and condemned as a hopeless heretic, against whom the Hapsburg King Philip II of Spain (1527–98) would launch a crusade, aided from within Elizabeth's own kingdom by English Catholics loyal to their supra-national spiritual authority. Scotland, a separate kingdom still, was aligned with the enemy, and Mary, Queen of Scots (1542–87) was the preferred Roman Catholic candidate to replace her cousin on the English throne.

Editorial control

There is evidence that, as early as 1563, Elizabeth and her advisers had taken steps to ensure that only approved portraits should be copied and circulated. We can assume that awareness existed in her circle of the way portraiture could be employed to reinforce authority, while at the same time defining, or at least characterising, that authority; the paintings by Hans Holbein the Younger (1497/8–1543) of Elizabeth's father, must have been well known. Henry, though, had been aggressively masculine, and appeared so in his portraits: bluff, bearded, foursquare, threatening. A subtler, more layered presentation would be needed to convey a positive message for Elizabeth.

NON SINE SOLE
IRIS.

We can see elements of the 'Virgin Queen' image in her early portraits, in the 1572 miniature by Nicholas Hilliard (c.1547–1619), for example, with its white eglantines; this was unsurprising, as she would have wanted to emphasise that she was available for marriage in the virgin state. This relatively obvious subtext later transforms into a pictorial depiction of the political advantages of being unmarried: Elizabeth is alone, not subject mind and body (as was her sister Mary I through her marriage to Philip II of Spain) to any foreign male control; Elizabeth gives herself in marriage to her country. The Virgin Elizabeth in her later images could be read as a substitute for the Virgin Mary, drawing on the love and loyalty due to such a revered figure or, to put it more crudely, hijacking a key Catholic icon.

Code-breaking

In a portrait painted around 1580, of which several versions exist, with the prime example now in Siena, Elizabeth holds a sieve. Why? Was she keen on gardening? To decipher this image, we must engage with the fashion of the time for emblematic communication, which makes many Elizabethan paintings a halfway house between text and image; intriguing codes to be broken only by those fully in the know. Casual and uninformed observers, as most of us are, must work hard to extract the full meaning, but we can still admire and appreciate the overall impression of power, majesty and purity conveyed by the more pictorial elements of the picture: the pose, background and colour scheme. The scholarship and communication skills of Sir Roy Strong, a former Director of the National Portrait Gallery, have revealed much of this. Strong explains that the sieve

Elizabeth I

Quentin Massys the Younger, 1583
Oil on panel, 1240 × 920mm (48⅞ × 36¼")
Pinacotecca Nazionale, Siena

Portraits were exchanged between European royal families as tokens of esteem and as visual documents in negotiations for marriage and other treaties. This one does not have a Sienese theme, but a Roman one, as Elizabeth I poses with her sieve like Tuccia the vestal virgin, who carried the water in her sieve from the River Tiber into the Vestal House. The Virgin Queen stands by a column on which a series of cameos tell the story of Dido and Aeneas: Elizabeth is to be seen as Aeneas, actively sailing away to found Rome, rather than passively succumbing to grief like Dido of Carthage. We are reminded by the globe that Elizabeth had imperial aspirations; although here we must acknowledge the role of influential advisers such as Sir Christopher Hatton and Sir Francis Walsingham, who pushed the anti-Spanish advantages of maritime adventure, and who may have had a hand in briefing the artists to produce images such as this. Several versions of this portrait exist, reminding us of the part played by the copying process in confirming the legitimacy of, and people's loyalty to, Elizabeth I.

Elizabeth holds can be read on two levels. It is first a symbol of discernment; she sifts through good and bad ideas and selects her ministers like any head of state. That much perhaps is guessable, but the hidden meaning is a reference to the Roman vestal virgin Tuccia, who carried water from the River Tiber into the Vestal House, in her sieve, without any spilling through. The subtlety of this allusion suffers in a laboured explanation, but most of the courtier class of Western Europe would have known their classical stories and would have needed no help with this.

The Sieve Portrait, then, is an emblem of Elizabeth's fitness to rule alone, symbolising her wisdom and, through her purity, her independence. But not quite alone. This portrait, according to Strong, reflects the agenda of many of the ambitious, anti-Spanish, ardently Protestant advisers close to her: men like Sir Francis Walsingham (c.1530–90) and Sir Christopher Hatton (1541–91). The presence of a globe in the Sieve Portrait refers to the ambition 'to enlarge the circumference of her dominion to include not only Britain and Ireland but some new world as vast as the universal frame . . .'. Imperial aspirations, no less, and they are restated in the Armada Portrait (see page 36), painted to commemorate the defeat of the Spanish invasion attempt in 1588. The globe, no longer a mere background accessory, now rests under her hand.

The global stage

The Gallery's famous Ditchley Portrait, so called because it commemorates Elizabeth's visit to Ditchley House in Oxfordshire in 1592, is a further escalation in the depiction of her power. She now stands upon the globe, spanning Heaven and Earth, an omnipotent virgin bride for her people. She enlightens the world, turns away from the darkness of strife and commands our allegiance, if not our worship. The image implies divine sanction for her monarchy, a theory articulated by her successor James I (1566–1625), whose conspicuous lack of success in persuading people to accept the divine right of kings had much to do with poor presentation. Elizabeth's visual image was an exaggeratedly positive affirmation both of her charismatic personality and of her political and dynastic situation.

A further potential weakness of Elizabeth's public self was that she was not only single, and therefore without a direct heir, but also ageing – she was fifty-five years old in 1588, the year of the Armada. The portraits disguised this process, presenting a pale mask surrounded by distracting masses of material and lavish jewellery, with many of the jewels conveying layers of meaning, further enhancing her power and mystery. The Rainbow Portrait, possibly commissioned by her minister Robert Cecil, first Earl of Salisbury (c.1563–1612), which still hangs in the house he built at Hatfield, dates from around 1600, and shows a youthful face belying her sixty-seven years (p. 31).

Who should have the credit for developing the brand 'Elizabeth I'? She must take much of it for herself, particularly for the theatrical dignity of her public appearances and the words she spoke at them; her appearance at Tilbury and her speech there on 8 August 1588, with England in danger of invasion, typifies so much that has been

Elizabeth I
Marcus Gheeraerts the Younger, c.1592
Oil on canvas, 2413 × 1524mm (95 × 60")
National Portrait Gallery, London (NPG 2561)

This portrait was commissioned by Sir Henry Lee to mark a visit by Elizabeth I to his house at Ditchley, in Oxfordshire. It was the centrepiece of a pageant in which Sir Henry expressed his remorse and regret at having slighted the Queen by going to live at Ditchley with his mistress, Anne Vavasour. The painting expresses both the cosmic splendour and earthly power of Elizabeth, and the particular gratitude – the sonnet refers to 'rivers of thanks' – Lee owes to the Queen for her anticipated forgiveness of him. The personal bond between female monarch and male subordinates, and the monarch's controlling role, are vividly demonstrated. There is little better evidence for how courtiers saw the Queen, or more realistically for the image of her they thought it politic to subscribe to. The ageing virgin still has a youthful figure and emphasises in her dress the mystic, bridal union with her country. She controls the pattern of the heavens, towering over her country and the globe: a pictorial assertion of her divine right to rule which is as effective as any of the wordy arguments of her successor James I.

Elizabeth I
Isaac Oliver, c.1590
Watercolour on vellum, 62 × 53mm (2½ × 2")
Victoria and Albert Museum, London

admired about her, and articulates the dedication and willing self-sacrifice that has characterised the most respected members of our royal family over the generations: '. . . I am come amongst you as you see at this time, not for my recreation and disport, but being resolved, in the midst and heat of the battle, to live or die amongst you all, to lay down for my God and for my kingdom, and for my people, my honour and my blood, even in the dust. I know I have the body of a weak and feeble woman, but I have the heart and stomach of a king, and of a king of England too.'

A host of admirers

On the visual side, we must also give credit to those around her, including the artists, both known and unknown. Elizabeth I did not take much interest in the visual arts, and if she liked pictures of herself, as Horace Walpole (1717–97) later said, it was more because she approved of the attention than because she appreciated the aesthetics. She did not collect paintings as some of her subjects were beginning to do, and gave few indications in conversation of any particular interest; many of the best-known images of her were commissions by courtiers and ministers, often with particular agendas, and with a more sophisticated interest in the visual arts

Elizabeth I known as The Armada Portrait
Attributed to George Gower, c.1588
Oil on panel, 1070 × 1350mm (42 × 53")
Woburn Abbey, Bedfordshire

In 1588 the Roman Catholic King Philip II of Spain sent an invasion fleet, an Armada, to crush the heretical Protestant Queen Elizabeth I. A combination of irresolute Spanish leadership, English naval skills, bad luck and bad weather delayed and eventually destroyed the 'Enterprise of England'. The portrait shows the destruction of the Spaniards by the weather and celebrates England's deliverance and Elizabeth's personal splendour. Once again, a globe hints at imperial ambitions.

ABOVE **The Armada Jewel**
Nicholas Hilliard, c.1588
Gold and enamel with diamonds and rubies
Overall height 70mm (2¼"), miniature
39 × 30.5mm (1½ × 1¼")
Victoria and Albert Museum, London

ABOVE RIGHT AND DETAIL
Sir Christopher Hatton (1540–1591)
Unknown artist, c.1589
Oil on panel, 781 × 654mm (30¾ × 25¾")
National Portrait Gallery, London (NPG 2162)

Hatton holds a cameo brooch depicting Elizabeth I,
asserting his love and loyalty in a typically courtly
way. Miniature painted portraits, cameos and symbolic
jewels were exquisite words in the language of
courtly discourse, given and received as tokens of
admiration, worn ostentatiously by even the older
courtiers; the elderly adviser Lord Burghley was
portrayed with a royal cameo in his hat. The Queen
loved jewels; her closest courtiers were expected
to keep her supplied with expensive and symbolic
items, and she wears a variety in her portraits,
providing a convenient shorthand identification:
the Phoenix Portrait, the Pelican and so on. The
Armada jewel has obvious connotations. The Queen
was a woman and her most powerful courtiers and
ministers were all men. The jewels, the miniatures
and the cameos, as well as the words and music of
the expressive arts, commented on this particular
phenomenon and its implications for the sexual
politics of the court and male/female relationships
in general.

than their sovereign. This particularly applies from 1590, when
Marcus Gheeraerts the Younger (c.1561–1636) and Robert Peake
(*fl.*1526–d.1626?) were prominent among artists exploring the
possibilities of the full-length portrait on canvas (a ground little
used in this country before 1580).

Nicholas Hilliard's scale and technique were a complete contrast,
retaining many of the skills of the medieval manuscript illuminators,
but in his use of a coded, courtly visual language he was a very
influential contemporary figure. He is the only artist with whom
Elizabeth is known to have conversed: he wrote of painting her out of
doors, in full light, because she abhorred shadows and because she
believed the Italians did not use them in their painting. A revealing
episode, if true: the necessary lighting conditions to produce the
'mask of beauty' as the sunlight reflected off her pale face, combined
with a striking ignorance of Italian art! Hilliard did much to create
her visual image: he had been working at the court certainly since
1570, predominantly as a miniaturist, but with occasional life-scale
work. It was his successor Isaac Oliver (d.1617), though, who produced
a sobering counterbalance to the rejuvenated and elaborate post-1580s
image. Oliver's unfinished miniature of the gaunt, ageing queen
(opposite page) cannot have met with her approval.

Elizabeth's image has retained its vigour and clarity: the pale
face, roman nose and high forehead crowned by reddish hair (approxi-
mated in later years by elaborate wigs) are immediate and imposing.
Austere yet vulnerable, there is none of the triviality of prettiness or
the distraction of great beauty: this is a face of character for a woman
of sovereign authority. It is easy to believe the description of the

A theme of film and TV portrayals has been the clash between personal feelings and public duty, the perennial problem of a monarchical system: Cate Blanchett's Elizabeth was too fond of her Earl of Leicester, Glenda Jackson's BBC Elizabeth resisted advice to marry, and matured magnificently over six episodes. Flora Robson, in contrast, embodied national defiance in *Fire Over England*, and Judi Dench displayed a resigned, imperious maturity.

OPPOSITE
Elizabeth I
Unknown artist, c.1600
Oil on panel, 1273 × 997mm (50⅛ × 39¼")
National Portrait Gallery, London (NPG 5175)

Painted some forty years after her coronation, this portrait may have been part of an attempt to rejuvenate the ageing Queen's image. It is a simple image: the pose is traditional and hieratic, obvious in its message and bland in its characterisation. Yet it has informed later characterisations of Elizabeth (see Cate Blanchett image, above).

seventeenth-century historian Isaac Fuller (1606–72): 'She had a piercing eye, wherewith she used to touch what metal strangers were made of who came into her presence . . . and counted it a pleasant conquest with her majestic look to dash strangers out of countenance.' This powerful personality, combined with the drama of her life, her pivotal role, and her dealings with a range of handsome, dangerous and clever men, have made her a cracking good part for several actresses of consummate skill: Bette Davis, Flora Robson, Glenda Jackson, Cate Blanchett and Judi Dench have all taken her on, helping generations of audiences towards an appreciation of the Queen and her era.

Power and performance

These performances may offend sticklers for factual exactitude, but because so much of monarchical power is itself a performance, a calculated presentation of the self through words, images, appearances and sanctioned narratives, and because this artifice carries a personal cost, the best performers tell us much that is true about that personal cost, conveying the private strain that underlies the public confidence; think of the resigned wisdom and weariness of Judi Dench's Elizabeth in *Shakespeare in Love*, a small part maybe, but a performance of measured depth. Even in the anachronistic knockabout of the TV series *Blackadder*, Miranda Richardson's emotionally immature, spoilt-brat queen has authentic echoes of Elizabeth's challenging haughtiness.

It does not diminish Elizabeth I to conclude that her visual image and the way that it perpetuates her memory were in a large measure the work of other people. The key contemporary images of her were reflections of how her courtiers thought she should be seen, often containing references to policies and events in which they themselves had a particular interest. We must remember that she employed no court painter dedicated to the promotion of her image; the 'Sergeant-Painter' George Gower (d.1596), in post from 1581 until the year of his death, and credited with the Armada portrait, comes nearest, but he had many other more mundane duties in and around the court. The substance of the image was the Queen herself, her courage, intellect, personality, and public manner; she focused the nation's aspirations, projecting through her person the courage and defiance of an embattled people, and confirming to her subjects their existence as an independent nation.

William Shakespeare

Shakespeare is the most celebrated, performed and studied playwright in the world. His name is synonymous with the English language and new interpretations of his plays continue to illuminate the human condition

When I was a child, I talked and talked, and when my teachers complained and my parents took me to task, my defence was that I had 'a lot to say'. The quality of what I said was, sadly, immaterial. I went on talking. But then, in the mid-1980s, I joined the Royal Shakespeare Company, and Shakespeare blazed into my life. He gave me other people's words to speak, and they were much better words — in fact, the best words of all. This discovery of Shakespeare's language and how it works has been the greatest discovery of my life.

Shakespeare has become famous for being famous. He is constantly misquoted. He is loathed by schoolchildren, who find him irrelevant. He has been hijacked by politicians, appropriated by vicars, overused by after-dinner speakers. His face seems washed out, lank and unattractive from appearing on too many banknotes for over twenty years. And yet he remains the greatest artist this country has ever produced.

So why is Shakespeare so great, and why should an artist become the Greatest Briton? The claim for the primacy of art is straightforward: art does nothing less than define the inner nature and condition of Man. The artist bears witness to what we are, not to what we should be. And no artist bears witness more effectively than William Shakespeare.

As W. B. Yeats (1865–1939) once observed, since human beings learned to stand, we have disgraced ourselves. Our behaviour has resulted in world wars, empire building and murderous ambition. And yet we human beings have also produced medical cures, works of art and the miraculous abstraction of our thought and feeling that is music. We are a strange pot-pourri of weakness, power and savagery; of hope, fear and nobility. No other writer gives voice to this continuous contradiction and variation in the human spirit with such compassion and efficiency of expression

as the glover's son from Stratford, William Shakespeare.

In his plays, Shakespeare captures the mystery of the individual in the world. No other writer in any language has been able to map our emotional DNA with such accuracy. He retold stories, reinvented old themes and always turned them upside down. He took language and ideas with all their effects, atmospheres and feelings and harnessed them to the human heartbeat. This was and remains his genius.

Shakespeare wrote of race, immigration, gender, money, power and its corruption — the same issues that fill our news-screens today. In his language we hear ourselves — sometimes elevated, sometimes debased. The extremity of our behaviour is still where we find out who we are. The line between barbarism and civilisation is very thin indeed: if we have learned anything, it is that we have not developed from one century to another. Civilisation is an attempt to cover our moral sweatiness like an antimacassar; and like an antimacassar, it is lace-thin. Moments of drama force us into taking the cover off.

Shakespeare's brilliant plots take people into situations that test their spirits — King Lear is rejected by his daughters and finds himself on a heath with a fool and a madman; Isabella finds herself weighing her virginity against the life of her brother; Bottom, a weaver, sleeps with a fairy queen. Miranda sees a boy for the first time and declares, 'Oh brave new world, that has such people in't'; her father wearily responds, as we might, ''Tis new to thee.' Shylock, an outsider, asks the eternal question of all outsiders: 'If you prick us, do we not bleed?'

There is not a question we wrangle with today that is not explored in Shakespeare's plays. And yet he supplies no answers. He does not tell us who we should be, merely who we are. This lack of legislation is repeatedly evident in his incidents of love. People in his plays fall in love without

William Shakespeare 1564–1616

1564	Born in Stratford-upon-Avon to a local glover, he is baptised on 26 April
1582	At the age of eighteen, Shakespeare marries 26-year-old Anne Hathaway
1585–92	Sometimes known as the 'lost years'. Shakespeare leaves Stratford to join a company of actors as playwright and performer. He writes his first play, *Henry VI*, in three parts
1592	Shakespeare is called an 'upstart crow' by Robert Greene and theatres in London are closed due to the plague
1593	Starts the first of his 154 sonnets. Christopher Marlowe is murdered in a brawl
1594	Founding member of the Lord Chamberlain's Men, a theatre troupe which includes the comic, Will Kemp, and the greatest tragedian of the age, Richard Burbage, who later portrayed Hamlet, King Lear and Othello
1595	*Romeo and Juliet*, *A Midsummer Night's Dream* and *Richard II* are published
1599	The Globe Theatre opens on Bankside with a performance of *Julius Caesar*. Shakespeare holds a ten per cent share
1601	The first of his great tragedies, *Hamlet*, is written. His father dies
1603	*A Midsummer Night's Dream* is performed before Elizabeth I. The company becomes The King's Men to honour the accession of James I
1611	Shakespeare returns to Stratford, moving into New Place. Supposedly writes *The Tempest* and *Cardenio* – his only lost play – this year
1616	Dies on 23 April and is buried at Holy Trinity Church, Stratford-upon-Avon
1623	John Hemminges and Henry Condell publish the First Folio, 36 of Shakespeare's 37 plays

explanation: he signals that love is a territory no one can govern, and where the consequences are often harsh. Romeo falls for the daughter of the enemy, and does so at first sight, as do Rosalind, Viola and Ophelia. These people merely cope with the mystery of their fate.

Shakespeare never falls into a mode of conveying wisdom. Kings are often fools and madmen wise; cross men speak with compassion; cool nuns are passionate; jokers are sad; even gentle universal truths such as 'All the world's a stage, and all the men and women merely players' are softened when the words are spoken by a maverick.

Each character in Shakespeare's plays speaks with an individual voice: it is as if Shakespeare took down what ordinary people said and then framed it. This process then transformed the experience of each character in the plays into universal speech, available for each generation to renew. By saying who we are we help to make ourselves free: a generation of psychotherapy is built on that premise. And the rhythm of the play becomes the key to the unconscious.

Shakespeare invented words and phrases that have expanded the language and have made English the envy of the world. He inherited a new grammar and an optimism that came with the rise of Elizabethan England and rode on the power of both to infect people with an excitement. He was a radical who did not offend, an anarchist who inspired. He has given us a language that needs to be spoken aloud. And when it is, it reminds us that language is physical and sexy and muscular, and that it empowers both speaker and listener. He invented words as his imagination burst through the bonds of the existing language, and those words have embedded themselves in the English that we speak today – both here and all over the world. His words have allowed us to think and feel at the same time with enviable subtlety. This is a gift that endures every day we speak or reach for the words that free us. The voices of Shakespeare's characters continue to explore the 'infinite variety' of humanity. His genius lies in capturing ours.

The image of an artist

'Shakespeare – the nearest thing in incarnation to the eye of God.'

<small>LAURENCE OLIVIER (1907–89)</small>

Joseph Fiennes starring as Shakespeare in
Shakespeare in Love, 1998

<small>OPPOSITE</small>
William Shakespeare
Martin Droeshout, published 1623
Engraving, 191 × 159mm (7½ × 6¼")
National Portrait Gallery, London (NPG 185)

The First Folio of Shakespeare's plays, the first
published edition, appeared in 1623 with an
engraving by Martin Droeshout. This image,
presumably commissioned by the editors and
sanctioned by Ben Jonson, has always carried
authority as an authentic likeness of Shakespeare.
It appeared in four 'states': the first, or proof, state
and second state for the First Folio; the third state
(as illustrated) for the Second and Third Folios of
1632 and 1664; and the fourth state for the Fourth
Folio of 1685. Its status and clarity of line have
led to numerous reproductions and imaginative
adaptations.

In the 1998 film *Shakespeare in Love* we meet Shakespeare as a sprightly,
streetwise young man, full of impish charm and blessed with a full
head of hair. Do we believe that Joseph Fiennes, giving a splendid
performance, has accurately presented the great playwright? Would
we have preferred something closer to the well-known image of the
bald burgher of Stratford? Certainly Shakespeare must have been
young once, and have had some hair, but there is no doubt that it
is easier to catch the spirit of Shakespeare, and his theatrical texture
and human legacy, than it is to fix on something so personal, so
precise as his appearance.

Man of mystery

Doubt surrounds the image of Shakespeare as much as it does the
authorship of his plays. Some of the attempts to express and resolve
these doubts have wandered along the wilder shores of scholastic
eccentricity, but they have still been compelling enough to command
attention. On 31 March 1992, for example, a leader in *The Times*,
entitled 'Bess Unmasked', discussed the findings of some American
computer analysts who had compared the well-known engraving
of Shakespeare (from the first collected edition of his works) with
portraits of all his contemporaries, and concluded that the best
match was with Elizabeth I. The tongue-in-cheek conclusion of the
leader writer was that the Queen had written the plays – she may
have had 'the body of a weak and feeble woman', but she also had
the wit and learning of a master hack, hiding this disreputable
accomplishment for a woman behind the face of a man. All good
fun, and made possible by the uncertainty and speculation that
already surrounds Shakespeare and his work.

What, then, do we know? That there are three contemporary or
immediately posthumous images of Shakespeare that have some
claim to authenticity; that all subsequent portraits of him are based

Shakespeare's monument in Holy Trinity Church, Stratford-upon-Avon, Warwickshire
Gheerart Janssen, 1623
By kind permission of Holy Trinity Church, Stratford-upon-Avon

The monument in Holy Trinity Church (above) and The Chandos Portrait in the National Portrait Gallery, London (p. 49), are the most accessible images of Shakespeare with claims to authenticity. The Stratford monument has the advantage of having been commissioned by friends and family and of residing in perpetuity in his home town. It suffered minor damage from vandals in 1973, and has collected some choice insults from visitors: 'goggle eyes', 'painful stare', 'gaping mouth', 'man crunching a sour apple', etc. Others have found clear indications of serenity and a sociable disposition.

on one of these three, or a blend of them; and that for distinct periods of our history, two of these originals have been the dominant images. We shall discuss each of the three images in turn, while bearing one general comment in mind: they are modest productions, in their plain simplicity unrepresentative of the towering genius of the playwright, and this has led succeeding generations to adapt and enhance those images in the hope of achieving a more appropriate result.

Limestone and plaster

The first image may possibly be the most authentic, but has nevertheless been the least reproduced of the three. This is the memorial statue in Holy Trinity Church, Stratford-upon-Avon, a half-length sculpture in painted limestone. It is believed that this was commissioned by Shakespeare's family, and it is attributed to the sculptor Gheerart Janssen, sometimes known as Gerard Johnson (fl.1616–23), one of an Anglo-Dutch family of tomb-makers based near the Globe Theatre on Bankside in London. It was in position by 1623, and these probable origins mean that it may therefore be a good likeness. It has not, however, generally had a good press: the American Washington Irving (1783–1859), recounting a visit to Holy Trinity in 1815, found 'the aspect cheerful and serene', but C. M. Ingleby (1823–86) in 1861 was reminded of 'a man crunching a sour apple'; more dismissive still was the great Shakespearean scholar J. Dover Wilson (1881–1969), who saw in it the archetypal 'self-satisfied pork butcher'. Samuel Schoenbaum, however, to whom I am indebted for these quotations, was inspired by the image and its location and associations to undertake his invaluable work, *Shakespeare's Lives* (1979).

This statue is perhaps too humble an image for an immortal bard. It has nevertheless been reproduced, both in three dimensions (the National Portrait Gallery has two plaster copies) and in two: as an engraving by the pioneering art historian George Vertue (1684–1756) in 1721, on beer-bottle labels for Flower and Sons, the Stratford brewers, and for a Shakespeare colouring book in the mid-1990s – the latter two both modest, commercial uses in tune with the statue's perceived status. It has also undergone, and been saved from, one unwelcome make-over by the Shakespeare editor Edmund Malone (1741–1812), who in 1793, in Schoenbaum's words, 'performed (as he thought) a public service by having it whitewashed to conform with

Cover illustration of First Folio: *Mr William Shakespeares Comedies, Histories & Tragedies* with engraving by Martin Droeshout, published 1623
The Queen's College, Oxford

John Hemminges and Henry Condell published the First Folio edition of Shakespeare's plays in 1623. The title page engraving of the playwright is the second 'state' of the image, the first being the proof state. It was one of the earliest books to carry a picture of the author, a device that has generated many important literary portraits over the ages. On the cover of many modern editions, the image has proved both functional and iconic.

his neoclassical canons of taste'. Thankfully it was later repainted and has been thus preserved to be enjoyed today.

The official likeness

'It was for gentle Shakespeare cut,' claimed Ben Jonson for the engraving, signed 'Martin Droeshout' (1601–c.1650), that appeared on the title page of the First Folio (the first collected edition of Shakespeare's plays) in 1623, and was reproduced in different 'states' for the three subsequent Folio editions of 1632, 1664 and 1685. Sanctioned by John Hemminges (1556–1630) and Henry Condell (d.1627), the editors of the First Folio, endorsed by Jonson and adopted by posterity, this image resonates. Unfortunately, it is, as has been said, 'a crudely executed likeness'. If Martin Droeshout was truly the artist, and if he was working from life, then he could have been no older than fifteen at the time. Surely the revered playwright deserved better than to have his memory perpetuated by the work of a callow apprentice? Quite so, says the researcher and biographer Mary Edmond, whose diligence has done so much to illumine our understanding of Shakespeare's image. She suggested in 1991, most plausibly, that the engraving had probably been produced by the boy's uncle, Martin Droeshout the Elder, and that he did not take the image from life, but may have been working from a lost portrait by Marcus Gheeraerts the Younger, painter of the portrait of Elizabeth I reproduced on page 35.

Whether by Droeshout the Younger or the Elder, however, we can safely refer to it as the Droeshout engraving, and if it is by the Elder, that only makes its ordinariness the more disappointing. Unremarkable as it is, it was nevertheless the standard image of Shakespeare for the seventeenth century, via the Folio editions. It was then eclipsed by the Chandos painting (discussed below), which was in general use during the eighteenth century. The Droeshout was then rediscovered, and many versions and derivations followed during the nineteenth. The most controversial of these has been the so-called Flower portrait, named after Edgar Flower, of the Stratford brewing family, who brought it to the attention of the Society of Antiquaries in 1895 (see page 53). Until 1986 the Flower portrait was thought to be based upon the Droeshout engraving, but Paul Bertram and Frank Cossa argue, in their 1986 article 'The Flower Portrait Revisited' for the *Shakespeare Quarterly,* that the Flower portrait precedes

David Garrick (1717–79)
Thomas Gainsborough, exhibited 1770
Oil on canvas, 756 × 632mm (29¾ × 24⅞")
National Portrait Gallery, London (NPG 5054)

Kenneth Branagh in *Henry V*, 1989

Shakespeare's plays are still a proving ground for serious stage actors. David Garrick did more than act: between 1750 and 1770, he spearheaded the elevation of Shakespeare to a national icon. He packed theatres, adapting plays and characters to suit his particular talent. In our day Kenneth Branagh has used cinema to make Shakespeare accessible: starry casts, sensitive treatment of the text and magnificent locations have attracted many newcomers to the plays.

the Droeshout image, and is in fact the original on which the Droeshout was based. Careful technical examination has confirmed that the Flower's panel is 'ancient' and that the barely legible inscription 'Willm Shakespeare 1609' could be genuine, but has also showed the presence of bitumen, which was not used as a dark pigment until the mid- to late eighteenth century. Examination has further revealed that the Shakespeare image is superimposed on a madonna and child. So the jury, in some senses, is still out. There is insufficient technical evidence to prove that the Flower portrait is a lost original, and the provenance – or history of its ownership – is non-existent before 1840, yet there is still enough in its favour to keep the mystery open. The Flower controversy is an excellent example of the intriguing, self-fuelling uncertainty that both bedevils and stimulates the hunt for Shakespeare's image.

A national treasure?

Some of the same uncertainty hangs over the National Portrait Gallery's painting known as The Chandos Portrait, acquired by the 1st Earl of Ellesmere (1800–57) from the collection of the 2nd Duke of Buckingham and Chandos (1797–1861) in 1848 and presented to the Gallery to initiate the collection in 1856. Its provenance is traceable back from the ducal connection through the reports of George Vertue to the Restoration actor Thomas Betterton (c.1635–1710), who had it from the poet and playwright William Davenant (1606–68). Davenant, who was something of a line-shooter when drunk, claiming to be both Shakespeare's godson and his illegitimate son, told Betterton that it had been painted 'by one John Taylor, a player', who left it in his will to Davenant. Mystery surrounded this Taylor until 1982, when the tenacious Mary Edmond discovered records proving the existence, at the right period, of an artist of that name. The National Portrait Gallery has accepted the attribution to Taylor, but precautionary doubt remains about the identity of the sitter because the Taylor–Davenant–Betterton link is insecure. This is necessary and appropriate scholarly caution; there is, however, sufficient correspondence between the Chandos and Droeshout images and the Janssen memorial sculpture for the authenticity of the likeness to be widely accepted.

In aesthetic terms, the best paintings and sculptures based on one of the original images of Shakespeare derive from the Chandos

LEFT **William Shakespeare** known as
The Chandos Portrait
attributed to John Taylor, c.1610
Oil on canvas, 552 × 438mm (21¾ × 17¼")
National Portrait Gallery, London (NPG 1)

ABOVE **William Shakespeare**
Ozias Humphry after The Chandos Portrait
Drawing, 410 × 335mm (16⅛ × 13¼")
Folger Shakespeare Library, Washington, DC

The gold earring in The Chandos Portrait surprises many people. Men wore them extensively in the sixteenth century, the most fashionable sporting elaborate dangling confections of pearls and jewels. This portrait was the first acquired by the National Portrait Gallery, in 1856. Its provenance gives it a reasonable claim to authenticity and the likely artist was a contemporary of Shakespeare. It is of workmanlike quality, and since the eighteenth century has vied with the Droeshout engraving as the most reproduced and adapted.

painting. One of the first examples of these is the portrait by the Dutchman Peter Borsseler (fl.1665–84), dated c.1670, and known as The Chesterfield Portrait after its eighteenth-century owner, the letter-writing 4th Earl of Chesterfield (1694–1773). It shows a baroque, expressive Shakespeare, in which the restrained Chandos head and shoulders have acquired a seated, fully limbed body at ease in an airy space. Several leading eighteenth-century artists, including Sir Joshua Reynolds (1723–93), also produced their own versions: Sir Godfrey Kneller (1646–1723) presented one to John Dryden (1631–1700), who, being a poet, thanked him in verse:

> *Shakespeare*, thy Gift, I place before my sight;
> With awe, I ask his Blessing e're I write;
> With Reverence look on his Majestick Face;
> Proud to be less; but of his Godlike Race.
> His soul inspires me, while thy Praise I write.

William Shakespeare known as
The Chesterfield Portrait
Peter Borsseler, c.1670
Oil on canvas, 127 × 120mm (5 × 4¾")
Shakespeare Birthplace Trust

During the mid-eighteenth century this portrait
belonged to the letter-writing politician, the 4th Earl
of Chesterfield. Probably painted around 1670 by
a Dutch artist, it upgrades the prosaic Chandos
portrait into something more baroque and engaging,
more suitable for a major cultural figure. It gives the
playwright some space to fill, and some relaxed yet
authoritative body language.

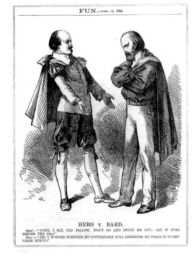

Hero v. Bard
William Shakespeare and Giuseppe Garibaldi
(1807–82)
Unknown artist, 1864
Wood engraving, 290 × 219mm (11⅜ × 8⅝")
National Portrait Gallery, London (NPG D13122)

Awe, reverence and majesty: with such an elevated status, it is small wonder Shakespeare's image needed an upgrade!

One further example enables us to restore some of the credibility of Edmund Malone, the whitewasher of the Janssen monument in 1793: an admirer of The Chandos Portrait, Malone obtained permission in 1783 for Ozias Humphry (1742–1810) to draw it. Pleased with the result, Malone noted on the back: 'The original having been painted by a very ordinary hand, having been at some subsequent period painted over, and being now in a state of decay, this copy, which is a very faithful one, is in my opinion, invaluable.' This copy is now in the Folger Shakespeare Library collection, Washington DC.

Malone's influential edition of Shakespeare, appearing in 1790, confirmed the rise in Shakespeare's reputation from the revered fellow professional of Dryden's encomium to unassailable patriotic totem. Two key factors lie behind this: France and David Garrick. Shakespeare's literary qualities became identified with British national characteristics – a vigorous, pragmatic flexibility, with strong elements of vulgarity – contrasting with French linguistic rigour, structural formality and refined distillation of aristocratic feelings. Voltaire fought bravely for Racine, Corneille and France, Samuel Johnson swung the British cudgels, but his friend David Garrick rode the white charger. Garrick's thespian and entrepreneurial skills,

Shakespeare and His Friends at the Mermaid Tavern
John Faed, 1850
381 × 467mm (15 × 18⅜")

In the nineteenth century, the image of Shakespeare benefited from the burgeoning popular interest in our national history. People delighted in romanticised narrative images of the playwright himself and in scenes from his plays. Other playwrights appeared in the supporting cast of this thespian pageant, but there was only one male lead. Christopher Marlowe, for example, suffering from the lack of editions of his plays, did not emerge fully until the mid-twentieth century.

if not his cavalier attitude to the texts, established Shakespearean performance as the criterion by which British actors would be judged.

The Chandos Portrait was also popular amongst Victorian history painters, meeting the demands of a public as avid for history paintings as we are for history on television. The Victorians took the Chandos face and attached it to a body involved in a variety of pageant-like contexts: *Shakespeare Contemplating His Characters*; *Shakespeare and His Friends at the Mermaid Tavern* (this picture includes John Donne, Francis Beaumont, John Fletcher, Francis Bacon and Ben Jonson); and, a more demanding assignment, *Shakespeare Reading* A Midsummer Night's

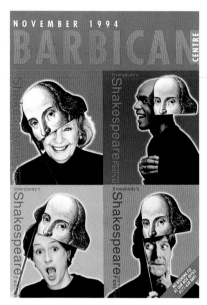

Barbican Centre pamphlet for 'Everybody's Shakespeare International Festival', 1994.

Today the identity of Shakespeare is indistinguishable from his drama. Yet he was a shrewd businessman too. By 1592 he was on the make in London, and five years later he bought New Place, a big house in Stratford. A sensible investor, he bought land, and held it as a gentleman, taking over the new family coat of arms on his father's death. He retired to New Place in 1611. The most celebrated English dramatist applied his worldly success conventionally, to acquire property and social status for the benefit of his family.

OPPOSITE
William Shakespeare, known as
The Flower Portrait
Unknown artist, date uncertain
Oil on wood panel, 570 × 440mm (22½ × 17⅜")
Copyright RSC Collection

This has a strong connection with the Droeshout engraving. Some scholarly opinion considers that it is original, copied by Droeshout for the First Folio engraving. Others think it is derived from the Droeshout, possibly as late as the nineteenth century. It is superimposed over a painting of a madonna and child.

Dream *to Elizabeth I*. These popular works provided an accessible image of Shakespeare both for the British domestic and imperial narrative, and – because many of them have crossed the Atlantic in the last hundred years – for the wider English-speaking world.

For the family

This popularisation of his image through narrative paintings was one aspect of the movement to render his plays and his personal history more suitable for a mass, and above all, a family audience. Thomas Bowdler offered *The Family Shakespeare* in 1807, twenty plays edited to be safe for, and intelligible to, the young and impressionable, although it was discovered later to be mainly the work of his sister Henrietta Maria. In the same year, Charles Lamb – with his sister Mary's contribution again not initially admitted – transformed twenty plays into prose stories, creating his *Tales from Shakespeare – designed for the use of young persons*. Safe access was thus provided for young feet to approach the national monument.

The cinema has widened the appeal of Shakespeare's plays, offering a new perspective to actors, directors and audiences. Baz Lurhmann has given us an exhilaratingly brash, urban American *Romeo and Juliet* (1997); Sir Ian McKellen's *Richard III* (1996) reeks of fascist brutality, minutely observed down to his 1930s vowel sounds. Sir Laurence Olivier and Kenneth Branagh have shown how productions of Shakespeare reflect the mood of a particular era: Olivier's wartime *Henry V* (1944) is a fantastical essay in colourful, gung-ho patriotism, while Branagh's (1989) muddy, bloody battle scenes are grimly realistic.

Reproductions and versions of the Droeshout and Chandos portraits continue to dominate the dissemination of Shakespeare's image. A survey of recent Shakespeare publications with an image of the playwright on the cover indicates that 'straight' reproductions of the two are used in about equal numbers. The covers of the New Cambridge Shakespeare editions, published by the Cambridge University Press, originally used a line drawing by Pablo Picasso (1881–1973), which was replaced by one by David Hockney in 1989. Both drawings were informed by elements of the Droeshout and the Chandos, and these consciously modern reworkings also conveyed the universality and timelessness of Shakespeare's contribution to human understanding.

Oliver Cromwell

Deeply religious, a brilliant soldier and
a shrewd politician, Oliver Cromwell was
instrumental in killing the King and turning
Britain into a republic. He ruled the country
as Lord Protector from 1653 to 1658

'Cromwell was a fine, self-taught soldier. He rose from obscurity . . . to preside over England's only republican government'
Richard Holmes, historian

There is no doubting his strength: his world-worn face looks out of the portrait by Robert Walker (c.1605/10–56/8) as if impatient with the theatrical props around. And there can be no denying his achievement. He rose from obscurity to play a key role in winning Parliament's victory in the English Civil Wars, and emerged from the turmoil to preside over England's only republican government. Though it failed to survive him, he had, as the historian J. H. Plumb declared in 1967, 'changed the course of British history; never again were royal absolutism and religious intolerance allowed to flourish unchallenged'.

Oliver Cromwell was born in Huntingdon on 25 April 1599, the only surviving son of a gentleman farmer. He was educated at Sidney Sussex College, Cambridge, leaving prematurely on his father's death in 1617. In 1620 he married Elizabeth Bourchier, daughter of a city merchant: it was a happy union, blessed with six children.

Although he became MP for Huntingdon in 1628, there is little evidence that Cromwell was initially a committed opponent of Charles I (1600–49), although family connections linked him to the opposition and he was certainly a religious radical, converted to puritanism. Elected to the Long Parliament in 1640 as MP for Cambridge, he supported its Grand Remonstrance – a statement of grievances against the authoritarian rule of Charles I – and later helped organise armed volunteers who prevented Royalists from seizing the Cambridge colleges' silver.

On the outbreak of civil war, he was soon advising Parliament to recruit 'men of spirit'. In 1643, the 'noble and active Colonel Cromwell' helped to secure East Anglia, and in July 1644 he made a major contribution to victory at Marston Moor. That autumn he pressed for vigorous prosecution of the war, supporting the formation of the New Model Army. He became lieutenant-general to its commander, Sir Thomas Fairfax (1612–71), uniquely retaining his MP's seat. His cavalry struck the decisive blow at Naseby in June 1645: Charles surrendered to the Scots in 1646, and was handed over to Parliament early the following year.

Cromwell advocated a settlement based on the monarchy. He argued that the army should not disband until terms were agreed with the King, but with Parliament deadlocked, he left Westminster for the army, and supported its Heads of the Proposals – a list of moderate demands compiled by senior officers including biennial parliaments, and religious toleration. It soon became clear that the army too was divided, with the Levellers demanding a shift in power and Cromwell taking a more conservative stance. In 1647 Charles escaped to the Isle of Wight, and the Second Civil War began, with Royalist risings and invasion by the Scots.

Cromwell was now sure that the King was untrustworthy, and held that ex-Parliamentarians who supported him were culpable 'because they have sinned against . . . so many evidences of divine providence'. After quelling a rising in Wales, he trounced the Scots at Preston in August 1648. When he returned to London in December 1648, he found that the army had excluded its opponents from Parliament, leaving only its so-called Rump in session, and over the following weeks he became convinced that 'the Providence of God' demanded that Charles should be tried for his life.

With the execution of the King in January 1649, Cromwell became a figure of prime importance, a member of the ruling Council of State. He was given command of the force sent to Ireland, now in arms for Charles II (1630–85): after first crushing the Leveller mutinies, he left for Ireland in mid-August 1649. His campaign was brutal, and has done much to damage his reputation. However, as Tom Reilly has shown in *An Honourable Enemy*, Cromwell's conduct at Drogheda and Wexford, where the Catholic garrisons were

Oliver Cromwell 1599–1658

25 April 1599	Born in Huntingdon into a wealthy family, named after Thomas Cromwell (c.1485–1540), who helped in the dissolution of the monasteries under Henry VIII
1616	Enters Sidney Sussex College, Cambridge
1640	Elected to Long Parliament as MP for Cambridge. Cromwell supports Parliament's grievances against King Charles I (1600–49)
1642	English Civil War starts; Cromwell raises troop of cavalry in Huntingdon for Parliament
1645	New Model Army is formed and Cromwell becomes Lieutenant-General. In June he helps beat the Royalists at the Battle of Naseby
June 1647	After failing to reconcile Charles I, Parliament and the army, Cromwell puts his full support behind the army
1648	Cromwell's army defeats the Royalists at the Battle of Preston and Cromwell eventually pushes for a full trial of Charles I, who was to be charged with treason
30 January 1649	Execution of Charles I. Cromwell's signature is third on the death warrant. The monarchy is replaced by the Council of State of the Commonwealth
	In August, he commands the army sent to crush Royalist forces in Ireland
1653	Cromwell, frustrated at the lack of political or religious reform, dissolves the Rump Parliament and is appointed Lord Protector of the Commonwealth
1654–57	Cromwell struggles to find a constitutional basis for government but rejects Parliament's offer of the crown in 1657
1658	Death of Cromwell – his son, Richard, succeeds him as Lord Protector
1660	The monarchy, under King Charles II, is restored to England
30 January 1661	Cromwell is exhumed, hanged and beheaded, and buried at Tyburn

killed in cold blood, was in accordance with the laws of war, and there was no massacre of civilians.

Cromwell returned to London before again setting off to confront the Scots, who had proclaimed Charles II as King. On 3 September 1650 he defeated them at Dunbar, and a year later smashed an invading army at Worcester. This left him the most powerful man in the land, but it was not until April 1653 that he despaired of achieving settlement with the Rump, and dissolved it. When the nominated assembly that followed – the Barebone's Parliament – collapsed in December 1653, Cromwell accepted a constitution, the Instrument of Government, and the title of Lord Protector. But his first Protectorate Parliament was a failure, and in 1655 Royalist uprisings encouraged him to divide England and Wales into districts, each governed by a major-general: this enhanced security, but identified him with military rule.

The second Protectorate Parliament produced the Humble Petition and Advice, which offered Cromwell the title of King. After pressure from the army he rejected it, though he accepted the new constitution. Early in 1658 he dissolved the fractious Parliament, and never called another.

His foreign policy was more successful, with the seizure of Jamaica and Dunkirk, though there were failures, notably in the West Indies. Cromwell died on 3 September 1658, and was succeeded as Lord Protector by his son Richard, but the Protectorate was unable to survive long without him.

Even those who detested Cromwell's politics could scarcely dispute the towering scale of his personality. The Royalist Earl of Clarendon (1609–74) saw him as an 'extraordinary man', endowed with 'a great spirit, and a most magnanimous resolution', while Sir John Reresby (1634–89), another Royalist, thought him 'one of the greatest and bravest men (had his cause been good) that the world ever produced'.

Cromwell was a fine, self-taught soldier, who mastered tactics and logistics and understood what makes men fight. As a politician he had no clear path to follow, and combined inaction, 'waiting on the Lord', with sudden action. When he was harsh, it was for a purpose, not from gratuitous cruelty. He was personally tolerant, and regretted failing to persuade his parliaments that religious toleration would not imperil stability. Love him or hate him, his greatness cannot be denied.

The image of a revolutionary

'Cromwell was a man in whom ambition had not wholly suppressed, but only suspended, the sentiments of religion.'

EDMUND BURKE (1729–97), British politician. Letter, 1791

Oliver Cromwell
Samuel Cooper, 1656
Miniature watercolour on vellum
70 × 57mm (2¾ × 2¼")
National Portrait Gallery, London (NPG 3065)

'A larger soul hath seldom dwelt in a house of clay'
John Maidstone, a member of Cromwell's household, c.1650

Was Cromwell the Great Beast, our one serious mistake in a thousand years of constitutional respectability, the creature from the black lagoon of anti-monarchist ideology, gorging on the blood of the saintly Charles I? Or was he one of the Elect, the agent of God's Providence, eventually rejected by a sinful, self-indulgent people in favour of the Babylonian Whore of the Stuart monarchy? If these don't fit, there are a myriad other interpretations: proto-liberal, proto-fascist, republican, closet monarchist, champion of religious tolerance, fanatical bigot, dissembling hypocrite, sincere Christian warrior, war criminal, racist, bully, loving father, nepotist, kill-joy, robust practical joker, God's instrument, cynical opportunist . . . .

Cromwell has been seen as all those things and more since he emerged from the mid-seventeenth-century English Civil Wars as the most prominent political and military personality of his time. He has come to personify that turbulent period, and his name has become a shorthand for later generations, as either a warning a celebration of what could be achieved: 'in Oliver's day', 'in Cromwell's time'. As recently as 1977, a Barnsley miner of republican views, refusing to celebrate the Queen's Silver Jubilee, stuck a placard in his window saying simply 'Oliver Cromwell'.

God's Englishman

'A larger soul hath seldom dwelt in a house of clay,' wrote his servant John Maidstone. The large soul is the key; it encompassed depths of passion, floods of impassioned rhetoric, inexorable waves of certainty and troughs of black doubt. Like the sea, it lacked definition, but its force was undeniable. In the three-and-a-half centuries since Cromwell's death, scholars and citizens alike have re-examined that soul and sought to interpret it – but full understanding of it still eludes us.

There is one strand of relative simplicity, which is his visual

These are contrasting images of power. Charles I's royal regalia, opulent surroundings, fine clothes, and a distant view of the sea bounding his island kingdom all contribute to an image of pacific authority. Cromwell's strength, conveyed by the baton of command, the armour and the attendant, rests on military and chivalric foundations.

image. Let us start out from the house of clay, in search of the soul. (We shall not find it, but the search might be good for our own.) We shall look at a sequence of images, using them as convenient pegs on which to hang some remarks about Cromwell's reputation across the centuries. Returning to his servant John Maidstone, what else has he to say about Cromwell's appearance?

> His body was well compact and strong, his stature under six feet, I believe about two inches, his head so shaped as you might see it a storehouse and shop, both of a vast treasury of natural parts . . . his temper was exceedingly fiery, as I have known, but the flame . . . was soon allayed with those moral endowments he had. He was naturally compassionate towards objects in distress, even to an effeminate measure . . .

Another contemporary, the politician and historian Philip Warwick (1609–83), having commented on Cromwell's general scruffiness, described him thus: '. . . his countenance swollen and reddish; his voice sharp and untunable, and his eloquence full of fervour . . .'.

Oliver Cromwell
Samuel Cooper, 1649
Watercolour on vellum
57 × 48mm (2¼ × 1⅞")
National Portrait Gallery, London (NPG 5589)

Oliver Cromwell
Samuel Cooper, c.1650
Watercolour on vellum
79 × 57mm (3⅛ × 2¼")
The Duke of Buccleuch & Queensberry, KT

Cooper painted both the earliest and the most intense portraits of Cromwell. His 1649 miniature has not been a source for other versions, but the c.1650 image has proved fertile. We engage directly with Cromwell, literally warts and all, in this powerful study of an intriguing man; further versions were made by Cooper, of much diluted intensity, and it seems likely that Sir Peter Lely based his portraits of Cromwell as Lord Protector upon it.

Significantly, Warwick also remarked that once he became a prominent public figure, Cromwell, 'having had a better tailor and more converse among good company', appeared 'of a great and majestic deportment and comely presence'. Something of a make-over, then, and entirely in keeping with the Protean nature of Cromwell: not just an East-Anglian bumpkin, but a shrewd operator who knew the political importance of personal appearance. This is reflected in his portraits.

Reading men's minds

No authentic portrait of Cromwell exists dated earlier than 1649, the year he emerged as Britain's leading military and political personality. There is a miniature by Samuel Cooper (1609–72) painted in that year, which may be a portrait of him, but, despite its obviously Cromwellian features (heavy face and unkempt hair with his particular pattern of balding), the sitter was identified as someone else until fifteen years ago. This is a fine image, but about a year later, Cooper produced another that has greater psychological intensity. Nowadays this image is much admired, conforming far more to what we expect of a portrait than many others of Cromwell. It seems to reflect an inner life of prayer, searching, doubt and irresolution; it has intensity and roughness; and the famous warts are literally present. We can engage through it with the unmasked Cromwell, projecting on to it all we have learned about this complex man. It is, in a sense, a very modern portrait, lacking the veneer of artifice that we see in others. It may have been intended as a pattern from which other, less revealing images, would be copied, such as the 1656 version on page 58. It is a Cromwell for us, in the idiom of portraiture that we nowadays prefer.

Cromwell's official image, however, was defined in 1649 by Robert Walker. Walker painted the leading Parliamentarians in a version of the style of Sir Anthony Van Dyck (1599–1641), providing a diluted and, to us, ironically mocking continuity in public portraiture from the regime of Charles I. Here we have Cromwell the soldier, with his attendant and his baton of command; it certainly flatters his appearance, if we take the later Cooper as our standard, but it is disappointingly uninformative about any of his military achievements. The armour is antique and rhetorical, alluding to generalised notions of chivalry rather than to the astonishing military achievements described by Richard Holmes.

Oliver Cromwell
Sir Peter Lely, 1653–4
Oil on canvas, 7750 × 6290mm (30½ × 24¾")
Birmingham Museums & Art Gallery

Cromwell needed portraits to confirm his status as Lord Protector. Sir Peter Lely made a significant contribution, establishing a sombre, more forceful image for the Protector than the diluted Van Dyckean efforts of Robert Walker. It is probable that Cromwell did not sit for Lely, but that the artist used Samuel Cooper's *c.*1650 miniature as his model. Lely's image, like all sanctioned, official portraiture, was much copied. An example of this process can be seen on page 69.

'Mr Lely, I desire you would use all your skill to paint my picture truly like me, and not flatter me at all; but remark all these roughnesses, pimples, warts, and everything as you see me…'
In Horace Walpole *Anecdotes of Painting*, ch. 1, vol. 3 (1763)

'Roughnesses, pimples, warts'

Walker almost certainly had sittings with Cromwell, but Sir Peter Lely (1618–80) probably did not. When Cromwell was installed as Lord Protector in December 1653, Lely was commissioned to make portraits to mark the event. It is strongly believed that Lely based his work on the Cooper miniature of *c.*1650, adding a little more hair and slightly lengthening the face. It is plain, and we can say that this plainness is a political statement, a puritanical eschewing of Van Dyckean elegance, with a simple moral authority replacing derivative glamour. Cromwell's famous 'warts and all' remark would seem to support this argument of conscious simplicity, although there is doubt as to whether he actually addressed it to Lely or to Cooper. His request should, though, be read not just as a personal dislike of flattery, but as a Protectoral brief for a distinct public face: 'I desire you would use all your skill to paint my picture truly like me, and not flatter me at all; but remark all

The Royall Oake of Brittayne

these roughnesses, pimples, warts and everything as you see me; otherwise I will never pay a farthing for it.'

The argument for and against Cromwell has been conducted in many different media. The Civil Wars and subsequent upheavals stimulated the production of political pamphlets and broadsheets, enlivened by satirical cartoons featuring prominent personalities. Cromwell first appeared in print in this way in 1646, and over the next twelve years a rich and allusive argument for and against his performance emerged. In the satirical engraving 'The Royall Oake of Brittayne' we see him as a regicide, standing over the jaws of hell as he orders the cutting down of the royal tree. In Holland, a mass of prints remind us of the European dimension of Cromwell's reputation in the 1650s; many of these feature a coarse, bullying Cromwell, a real power and a threat to Dutch trade, but doomed to destruction. Prints could be used for propaganda as well; 'The Embleme of England's Distractions…', issued in the year of his death, proclaims the pacific, godly basis of his regime.

The Royall Oake of Brittayne
Unknown artist, c.1649
Line engraving, 186 × 248mm (7⅜ × 9¾")
National Portrait Gallery, London (NPG D1322)

Clement Walker, a moderate Parliamentarian MP who was opposed to Cromwell and the army's militant anti-royalism, published this engraving. We see Cromwell telling his servants to 'kill and take possession', as he stands over the jaws of hell, a 'locus lubricus', a slippery place. The tree is destroyed, and with it all laws and liberty; the swine, the people of England, appear to gain nourishment, but are 'fatted for the slaughter'. Biblical and Latin quotations sanction Cromwell's destructive actions.

This presents Cromwell as bringing peace and
stability to the three kingdoms. The Angel Fame
trumpets his glory, the Dove of Peace flies overhead,
while beneath his feet he crushes the Whore of
Babylon – a metaphor for the Roman Catholic
Church whose seductive immodesty had attracted
Charles I. Biblical references surround him, in word
and image, mainly alluding to peace emerging from
war, for example, swords into ploughshares, spears
into pruning hooks.

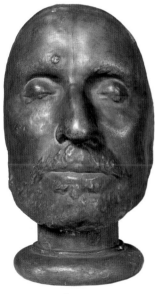

The existence of so many death masks is one
measure of the spell cast by Cromwell's reputation.
One of the most authentic, probably made some
ten to fourteen days after his death, is held by the
Ashmolean Museum; the one illustrated was cast
from it. Experts tell us that the excess of facial hair
can partly be accounted for by posthumous growth.

His severed head

The restoration of the Stuart monarchy in 1660 ensured that for the
next century Cromwell would be remembered as a villain as black
as Guy Fawkes. His body was exhumed in 1661 and his head severed
and displayed until 1684. The head was then sold and re-sold, exhibited as a curiosity, poked about by scientists and antiquarians, and
finally laid decently to rest at his old Cambridge college. This grisly
fascination is paralleled by the continual emergence of versions of
his death masks, regularly produced until the early 1900s. Cromwell
soon became an ogre in royalist folk-memory but the Earl of Clarendon,
a faithful servant to both Charles I and Charles II and the first historian
of the Civil Wars, recognised Cromwell's power abroad ('. . . it was
hard to discover which feared him most, France, Spain, or the Low
Countries . . .'), and gave this surprisingly balanced summary of one
of his masters' greatest enemies:

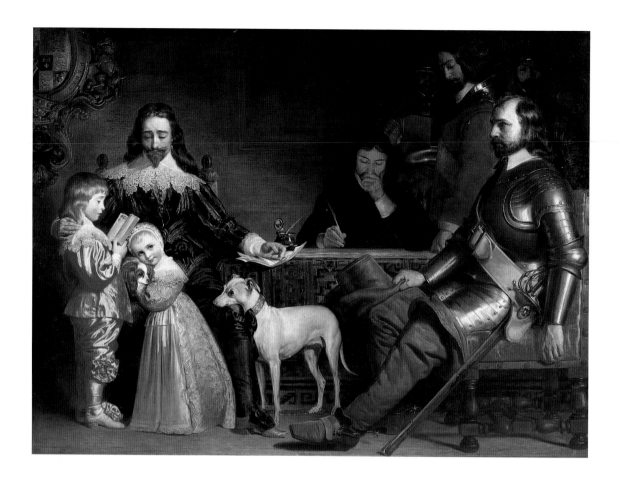

In a word, as he had all the wickedness against which damnation is denounced, and for which hell-fire is prepared, so he had some of the virtues which have caused the memory of some men in all ages to be celebrated; and he will be looked upon by posterity as a brave, bad man.

In the eighteenth century, Cromwell fell foul of the secular, rational minds of the Enlightenment. The philosopher and historian David Hume (1757–1838) dismissed him as a 'fanatical hypocrite', and a 'barbarian', believing that political Puritanism was 'full of fraud and ardour'. The historian Catherine Macaulay (1731–91) castigated him as 'the most corrupt and selfish being that ever disgraced a human form'. The only consistently positive comment was on his vigorous foreign policy, compared favourably with Hanoverian weakness in the 1720s and 1730s. In 1739 an engraving was issued, based on a Dutch medal of 1654–5, in which the ambassadors of Spain

An Interview between Charles I and Oliver Cromwell
Daniel Maclise, *c.*1836
Oil on canvas, 1842 × 2350mm (72½ × 92½")
National Gallery of Ireland

ABOVE **Cromwell on his Farm**
Ford Maddox Brown, 1874
Oil on canvas, 1430 × 1043mm (56¼ × 41")
Lady Lever Art Gallery, Port Sunlight

Cromwell, melancholy and soul-searching, Bible at the
ready, wonders if the wrath of God will burn like fire.
Ford Maddox Brown reprises the depressed mood of
his more famous *The Last of England* (1853), finding in
Cromwell's inner struggles of the early 1630s an echo
of his own emotional predicament.

ABOVE RIGHT
The Night before Naseby
Augustus Egg, 1859
Oil on canvas, 1016 × 1270mm (40 × 50")
Royal Academy of Arts, London

From the 1830s there was a history boom. Narratives
and novels such as those by Walter Scott, Thomas
Macaulay and Agnes Strickland became bestsellers.
The English Civil Wars were a favourite topic for both
writers and artists. Betweeen 1820 and 1900, some
175 paintings on Civil War topics were displayed at
the Royal Academy. Many Victorians saw themselves
perpetuating crucial political liberties, won in the
seventeenth century through a principled struggle
with Cromwell in the vanguard. The added romance,
drama and internecine tragedy of a civil war, added
a delectable, sensationalist frisson to a worthy
narrative.

and France argue about who should first kiss the graphically
depicted Protectoral arse.

The hero of British radicalism

It was in the mid-nineteenth century that Cromwell's reputation
was picked up, dusted off and explored in all its complexity. In 1845
the historian and essayist Thomas Carlyle (1795–1881) published for
the first time an edition of Cromwell's *Letters and Speeches*, accompanied
by an enthusiastic commentary. In effect, Carlyle allowed Cromwell
to speak for himself. At this time, there was a growing interest in
our national history, stimulated by popular scholarship, plays and
history painting, accompanied by an intense antiquarian interest
in original documentary material and thriving on strong narrative
involving dramatic personal encounters. In this Romantic reaction
against the coolness and detachment of the Enlightenment, Cromwell,
disinterred by Carlyle, became a hero of British political radicalism,
widely admired for exercising power with morality. Far from being
derided as a hypocrite, he became a role model for zealous, reforming,
non-conformist evangelicals. He appeared in dozens of paintings as a
godly hero: singing hymns at Dunbar; in a cavalry charge at Marston
Moor; praying, as in the 1859 *The Night before Naseby* by Augustus Egg
(1818–63); or bathed in moonlight and undergoing a Christ-like
agony in the garden in *The Death of Cromwell* (1867) by David Wilkie
Wynfield (1837–87), an exercise in saintly iconography.

Oliver Cromwell
Thomas Simon, 1653
Silver medal, 38mm (1½") diameter
National Portrait Gallery, London (NPG 4366)

Cromwell, 1970
Richard Harris stars as Cromwell with
Alec Guinness as King Charles I

OPPOSITE
Oliver Cromwell
After Samuel Cooper, 1656 or later
Oil on canvas, 222 × 165mm (8¾ × 6½")
National Portrait Gallery, London (NPG 588)

In an age still uneasy about the regicide of Louis XVI (1754–93) in the French Revolution, the more distant fate of Charles I was a safe surrogate for revisiting the issue obliquely, leading to – amongst many others – *An Interview between Charles I and Oliver Cromwell* (1836) by Daniel Maclise (1806–70), and, by the Frenchman Paul Delaroche (1797–1856), *Cromwell Gazing at the Body of Charles I* (1831). All these history paintings were, and still are, splendidly accessible and memorable; they were the visual idiom through which mass interest in British history was conveyed, perhaps too unconsciously anachronistic for our taste, but as important then as televised history is today for stimulating interest in Great Britons.

Military power and politics

The world was disfigured in the twentieth century by the military dictators of Europe, and Cromwell's reputation in the 1930s and 1940s suffered by comparison; W. C. Abbott, editing Cromwell's *Writings and Speeches* (1937–47), specifically compared him in his commentary to Mussolini and Hitler. In our present, more peaceful age, his association with military power in general, and specifically its application to political situations, has not worked in his favour; even less has the bloodshed of his Irish campaign of 1649, all too easily invoked to add fuel to the fire of more recent violence there. In the 1970 film, *Cromwell*, Richard Harris portrayed him as sensitive, thoughtful and resolute, but lacking the elemental force; in the Kevin Brownlow/ Andrew Mollo film *Winstanley* (1975), an earnest account of the Digger movement, a rough, unpolished Cromwell briefly appears, played by Bert Parnaby, skilfully contrasted with Jerome Willis as a gentlemanly Thomas Fairfax.

To end on a positive note, the recent celebration of the four hundredth year since Cromwell's birth in 1599 demonstrated the full extent of our continuing efforts to understand him. Many of the events were organised by the Cromwell Association and the very active Cromwell Museum at Huntingdon; associated publications and the resonant 'Oliver Cromwell's Internet Portal' have continued the themes. The whole exercise was characterised by that happy fusion of scholarly endeavour and popular, leisure-time participation that marks the best popular history and allows us to set our Great Britons in their own historical contexts, without being too precious to measure them against our present-day view of the world.

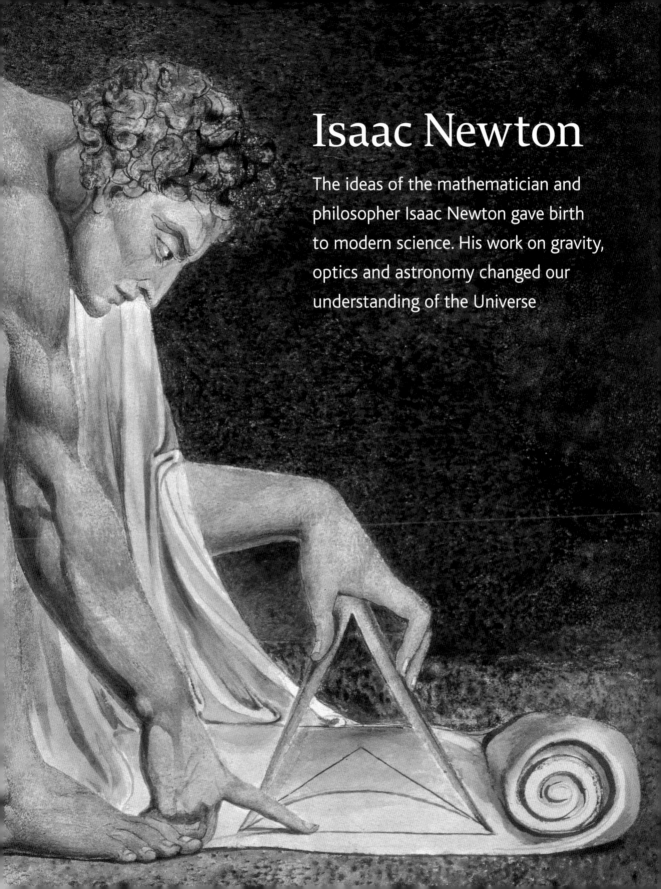

Isaac Newton

The ideas of the mathematician and
philosopher Isaac Newton gave birth
to modern science. His work on gravity,
optics and astronomy changed our
understanding of the Universe

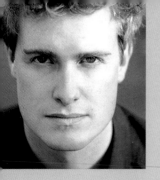

'Newton formulated nothing less than a coherent system of the world . . . an explanation still valid today'

Tristram Hunt, historian

The staggering contribution of Isaac Newton to human knowledge is difficult to overstate. In a life of incredible productivity and sheer unbridled genius, Newton formulated nothing less than a coherent system of the world. He provided a complete account of the structure and motion of the universe. From the movements of coastal tides to the trajectory of a comet, from the fall of an apple to a lunar eclipse, from the colour of a sunset to the planetary motion of Saturn, Newton supplied the explanation. An explanation still valid today.

Born on Christmas Day 1642 at Woolsthorpe Manor in Lincolnshire, amidst the chaos of the English Civil Wars, Newton's passion for knowledge and astonishing technical ability rapidly earned him the opprobrium of his Grantham schoolmates. Yet thankfully his teacher spotted the germs of genius and persuaded Newton's uninterested mother to put her son forward for university. Newton entered Trinity College, Cambridge, in 1661 and immersed himself in the study of geometry, mathematics and natural philosophy. Showing little interest in the official university syllabus, he pursued his own studies with what John Maynard Keynes (1883–1946) described as 'his unusual powers of continuous concentrated introspection'.

Newton's first interest was the study of optics. He became fascinated by the nature of light and the mechanics of vision – so much so that he began to carry out dangerous experiments on himself. One day, Newton slipped a bodkin 'betwixt my eye and ye bone as near to ye backside of my eye as I could' in order to test his theory of colours. Through a series of more prosaic experiments, involving two prisms and a ray of sunlight, Newton had overturned centuries of established thinking by proving that colour was not a mixture of light and darkness – on the contrary, sunlight was in fact a mixture of different colours. Furthermore, these colours (violet,

indigo, blue, green, yellow, orange and red, as we now conventionally identify them) travelled at different speeds and could be separated by refraction through a prism. This was a phenomenal discovery – according to Newton, 'the oddest if not the most considerable detection which hath hitherto been made in the operations of nature'. Once you understood sunlight, it was possible to explain the blue of the sky, the red of a sunset and the multi-colours of a rainbow.

In 1665 the plague hit Cambridge, and with the university closed, Newton returned to Woolsthorpe. Over the next two years, at this rambling country estate, the foundations of Newton's scientific genius were laid. Still not twenty-five, he turned over in his mind his four years of reading at Cambridge and after deep cogitation established the formula for calculus, one of the fundamentals of modern mathematics. By working out how to measure the gradient of a curve at a specific point, Newton could then generalise to the entire curve. From that, Newton was able to calculate precise rates of change over time. Today, calculus is an invaluable mathematical tool used in everything from construction to electrical engineering to speed cameras to cost-benefit analyses.

At Woolsthorpe, another thought struck Newton. According to his contemporary biographer John Conduitt (1688–1737), 'he was musing in a garden [when] it came into his thought that the power of gravity (which brought an apple from the tree to the ground) was not limited to a certain distance from the earth but that this power must extend much farther than was usually thought. Why not as high as the moon said he to himself . . . ' Yet the apple only really hit home twenty years later, when Newton collated his thoughts into *Philosophiae Naturalis Principia Mathematica*.

This work, more widely known simply as the *Principia*, is arguably the greatest book in the history of science. By correcting the work of Galileo Galilei (1564–1642),

Isaac Newton 1642–1727

25 December 1642	Born in Woolsthorpe, Lincolnshire
1655	The headmaster of Grantham School spots Newton's talent and he is sent to Trinity College, Cambridge, in 1661
1665	During the plague, Newton returns to Woolsthorpe where he conducts prism experiments and discovers the spectrum of light. He also works out his system of 'fluxions', precursor of the modern calculus, and considers the idea of gravity
February 1669	Newton describes his reflecting telescope in a letter to Henry Oldenburg (1619–77), first Secretary of the Royal Society
October 1669	Newton is elected Lucasian Professor of Mathematics and in January 1670 delivers the first of his Optical Lectures
1672	In February Newton publishes his letter on Light and Colours in the *Philosophical Transactions*; it is arguably the first scientific article
December 1680	Newton begins to observe the comet of 1680–81; he writes *Geometrica curvilinear*. In 1682 Newton observes Halley's comet
1684	Newton completes his calculations on gravity and shares them with Edmond Halley (1656–1742), who urges him to publish. The complete *Principia* is published in 1687
1699	Newton becomes Master of the Royal Mint
1703	Newton is elected President of the Royal Society
1712	Royal Society commission, under Newton's direction, investigates the competing claims of Leibniz and Newton to have developed calculus, and decides in favour of Newton
20 March 1727	Death of Sir Isaac Newton in Kensington, London

Johannes Kepler (1571–1630) and René Descartes (1596–1650), Newton founded the laws of motion that continue to underpin classical physics. The first was the law of inertia, which stated that bodies continue in uniform motion unless compelled to change by other forces; the second stated that the acceleration of an object is equal to the net force on the object divided by the object's mass; and the third stated that for each action (for each physical force) there is an equal and opposite reaction. Armed with these laws of motion and his formula for calculus, Newton returned to his apple.

The falling apple of Woolsthorpe (legendary or not) inspired Newton to think about gravity extending from the earth (where the apple fell to the ground) to the solar system (where the moon orbited the earth). Newton's genius was to suggest that the same force that attracted the apple to earth attracted the moon around the earth, and the earth (as well as the other planets) around the sun. In fact, every body in the universe (apple, moon, planet) is attracted to every other body by the force of universal gravitation. But he also discovered that the force of gravity decreases in an inverse square relationship with distance. The moon 'falls' or orbits the earth so much slower than the apple because it is so much further away from the earth's gravitational pull. And yet it never hits the earth, as the contrary pull of other celestial bodies manages to keep the moon in orbit.

In short, Newton had worked out the laws which govern the universe. With these, he could explain so much of what had hitherto been regarded as inexplicable freaks of nature or acts of God, from the trajectory of a comet to the rise and fall of the tides (as attracted by the gravitational pull of the sun and the moon). From the dark ages of fear and confusion, Newton began the process of enlightenment.

Across Enlightenment Europe, Newton was celebrated as the father of rationalism. His brilliant insights had undercut centuries of muddled thinking supported only by the power of custom. He was also feted for his belief in experimental observation. Unlike many of his scientific peers, Newton declared he would 'feign no hypotheses' and instead propound only what was clearly proven by experiment. Though inspired by Francis Bacon (1561–1626), Newton truly initiated the British tradition of dogmatic empiricism that remains at the heart of our academic, political and legal cultures.

Despite centuries of scientific progress, despite the splitting of the atom and the theory of relativity, the intuitive brilliance of Newton's discoveries remains startling and profoundly relevant.

The image of a scientist

'And make us as Newton was, who in his garden watching
The apple falling towards England, became aware
Between himself and her of an eternal tie.'

W. H. AUDEN (1907–73), 'O Love , the interest itself' (1936)

Woolsthorpe Manor, near Grantham, Lincolnshire

In the summer of 1665, Newton left plague-ridden Cambridge for the quiet of Woolsthorpe. As he later recalled, his observation of a falling apple led to questions about the nature of gravitational force. Thus the location became associated with the myths surrounding his creative thought and alleged patriotic, rustic simplicity. Woolsthorpe was given to the Royal Society, who passed it on to the National Trust during the Second World War.

OPPOSITE
Sir Isaac Newton
Sir Godfrey Kneller, c.1689
Oil on canvas, 972 × 686mm (38¼ × 27")
Portsmouth Estates

'Users get the pip as Apple knocks Newton on the head.' This jaunty headline, appearing in *Computer World*, announced the demise of Apple Macintosh's 'Newton' range of computers in 1998. Sir Isaac's reputation as a godfather of science continues to attract marketing people, and the myth of his apple flourishes as vigorously as the many trees planted in the grounds of academic communities, some of which claim lineal descent from the original at his birthplace.

The apple episode has been a powerful vehicle for conveying Newton's reputation. It carries simple, powerful, accessible meaning: the falling fruit observed by the graduate student – a banal occurrence in a country garden – becomes an emblem for the very process of scientific creativity. It's gravity, innit? Make the apple fall on his head and the simplicity, enhanced by humour, is the more memorable.

Eureka! – instant mythology

But is the story true? Its origins are certainly impeccable, as they go back to Sir Isaac himself. There is good evidence that he narrated the incident at least four times to different people during the last years of his life. This would suggest that it was important to him and that he wished it to be perpetuated. On 15 April 1726, after dinner, the antiquary William Stukeley (1687–1765) sat with Newton under some apple trees:

> ... he told me, he was just in the same situation, as when formerly, the notion of gravitation came into this mind. It was occasion'd by the fall of an apple, as he sat in contemplative mood. Why should that apple always descend perpendicularly to the ground, thought he to himself. Why should it not go sideways or upwards, but constantly to the earth's centre?

No, it did not fall on his head, but the rest is there as an easily transmittable and transmutable account, a ready-made myth; an

ISAACVS NEWTONVS.

Sir Isaac Newton
Charles Jervas, c.1717
Oil on canvas, 1257 × 1016mm (49½ × 40″)
The Royal Society

The portraits by Jervas and Vanderbank both remind us
of Newton's Presidency of the Royal Society from 1703
to 1727. Newton donated the Jervas to cement his
association with the Society, and the Vanderbank,
showing a vigorous, 83-year-old Newton, was widely
copied and engraved for the frontispiece of the third
edition of the *Principia*.

Bank of England £1 note depicting Sir Isaac Newton
Designed by Harry Eccleston, issued 1978
Reproduced by permission of the Bank of England

Archimedes moment for the Romantics who liked their flashes of
genius; a simple parable for Victorian improvers, ferreting out from
among the socially ill-favoured examples of achievement and
promoting them, *pour encourager les autres*; a visual slogan for modern
educators and marketers, saying, 'Look, Science is not scary at all,
there was this bloke by an apple tree . . .' But the evidence supports
a view that Newton launched the myth. At the time of his dinner
with Stukeley, he was 83-years-old, a distinguished public figure,
President of the Royal Society and Master of the Royal Mint, well
aware of how to inflate the 'bubble reputation', as we can see from
his attitude towards his own portraits.

A metropolitan genius

Two years after the publication of the *Principia* in 1687, Newton
commissioned a portrait from the most fashionable painter of the
day, Godfrey Kneller (1646–1723). After twenty years at Trinity
College, Newton was emerging as both a Cambridge and a London
celebrity, his status much enhanced by the *Principia* as well as by
involvement with the Royal Society, opposition to the interference
of King James II (1633–1701) in Cambridge University affairs, followed
by his election as MP for the university. It was Newton's desire to
assert his consequence that led him to Kneller's studio. The portrait
was, for 150 years, less well known than other works by Kneller,
but it is now widely reproduced. The Isaac Newton Institute of
Mathematical Sciences, opened in 1992, commissioned the painter
Barrington Bramley to copy it; the copy was unveiled on the
Institute's opening day by Sir Michael Atiyah, the inaugural Director
and, as Master of Trinity College and President of the Royal Society,
a thoroughly Newtonian figure. (On the same occasion, Lady Atiyah
planted an apple tree.)

The 1689 Kneller portrait gives us an apparently uncluttered
Newton: plainly dressed, with a full head of his own hair, intense
and abstracted, an uncompromising, rigorous and unworldly thinker
– an appropriate household god for an academic community.

In its apparent simplicity, it is easy for later generations to project
interpretations upon this portrait. One Victorian, keen on propagating
uplifting tales of geniuses from modest backgrounds, the better to
encourage popular striving, saw 'a yeoman's son' with 'a brow that
could measure the universe'. It speaks more eloquently to us, in search

Sir Isaac Newton
John Vanderbank, *c*.1725
Oil on canvas, 1270 × 1016mm (50 × 40″)
The Royal Society

Sir Isaac Newton
Possibly after John Michael Rysbrack, after 1727
Iron cast of death mask, 197 × 146mm (7¾ × 5¾″)
National Portrait Gallery, London (NPG 2081)

Death masks were powerful commemorators.
This is a cast from Rysbrack's, which he took
directly from Newton.

of our Shakespeare of science, than other portraits by Kneller and his contemporaries painted later in Newton's lifetime. These tend to be the self-promoting products of his subsequent celebrity, assertions of his power and status, often connected with the institutions that he controlled. The National Portrait Gallery's Kneller, painted in 1702 and widely reproduced in engravings, is subtly more worldly (p.81); by then Newton, having left academia for metropolitan distinction, had proved himself a ruthlessly effective Master of the Royal Mint; he now engages us directly as a manager should, plumper-cheeked and modishly perruqued. Kneller's 1720 portrait, both in its commissioning and in the presentation of the sitter, shows Newton as a consummate operator in managing his reputation: the French mathematician Pierre Varignon (1654–1722) was keen to have a portrait of his English hero, but Newton had been refusing to co-operate because of Varignon's association with scholars who supported Gottfried Leibniz (1646–1716) in the prolonged dispute over who was the first to invent calculus. In 1720, though, Newton, assiduously cultivating cross-Channel opinion, the better to launch a deluxe French edition of his *Opticks*, now agreed to Varignon's request.

Newton's relationship with the institutions in his life was consolidated through portraiture. He was active in ensuring that the Royal Society displayed and disseminated appropriate images, either by donating his own portraits or agreeing to sittings; in 1725, John Vanderbank (1694–1739) depicted the 83-year-old President, by then an incontinent invalid, as a sturdy, crimson-clad scholar, and this much-reproduced image became an eighteenth-century standard.

Inspiration beyond the grave

Newton died in 1727, but the posthumous image industry ensured him a variegated immortality. As in much of this piece, I here follow the interpretation of Dr Patricia Fara, whose *Newton: the Making of a Genius* (Macmillan, 2002) is a model of accessible, analytical scholarship. She establishes that Newton's eighteenth-century reputation was the product of many individuals and groups following particular agendas. There was no co-ordinated, centralised, government-led initiative, but an aggregation of individual enterprise, mostly entrepreneurially driven, producing, for a vibrant marketplace, an amazing range of Newton artefacts: paintings, engravings, busts, medallions and coins, both crude and cultured, for the assembly rooms, parlours, drawing rooms, lecture halls and schoolrooms of an autodidactic society.

In the eighteenth century, natural philosophy (Newton was not a 'scientist'; the word was not coined until a century after his death) became fashionable and commodified. Following the lead of Newton's disciples and the promoters of the British Enlightenment, the self-improvers consumed the products provided by Newton's commemorators and interpreters, prompted to revere him as, at first, one among many intellectuals and public men who were taking Britain to the top of the European league, with a measurable increase in his reputation as the century progressed.

Rational pride

In 1717 Newton's niece, Catherine Barton, married John Conduitt, a protégé of Newton and his successor as Master of the Royal Mint. Conduitt assumed immediate responsibility for the sacred flame of Newton's reputation, commissioning the eloquent monument that stands to this day in Westminster Abbey. The spin-offs from this monument, in terms of illustrated articles in journals, reproductions in engravings and medals and commentaries in sententious verse and grandiose nationalistic rhetoric, rendered it a key Newton icon. 'This grand and magnificent monument, erected to real merit, is a greater honour to the nation, than to the great genius for whom it was raised; and in this light it is viewed by all Europe.'

Conduitt was also responsible for a more subtle and enchanting commemoration, in the form of the 1732 painting by William Hogarth (1697–1764) known as 'The Indian Emperor'. In this, a children's performance of Dryden's play of that name, staged in Conduitt's town house, is watched by some of the royal children, a prestigious social coup. Gravity, in all senses, is represented by the bust of Newton by John Michael Rysbrack (1694–1770), in solemn isolation above the royals, with portraits of John and Catherine Conduitt in attendance to one side. In the background can be discerned Dr John Desaguliers (1683–1744), another Newton protégé and energetic populariser, a career he began under Newton's direct encouragement, delivering, for example, twenty-one interpretative lectures in 1713 alone. And a little child's fan has fallen, apple-like, to the ground.

Owen MacSwinny (d.1754), an Irish entrepreneur, impresario and

Monument to Sir Isaac Newton in Westminster Abbey
B. Cole, after William Kent and John Michael Rysbrack, after 1731
Line engraving, 251 × 169mm (9⅞ × 6⅝")
National Portrait Gallery, London (NPG D13121)

A performance of 'The Indian Emperor or The Conquest of Mexico by the Spaniards'
William Hogarth, c.1732–5
Oil on canvas, 1310 × 1467mm
(51½ × 57¾")
Private collection

This charming painting shows Rysbrack's marble bust of Newton presiding over a juvenile performance of a play by John Dryden, to an audience of royal children. It takes place at the house of John Conduitt, Newton's son-in-law and his successor at the Royal Mint, who, like his wife, looks down from a portrait.

BELOW RIGHT **Allegorical Monument to Sir Isaac Newton**
Giovanni Battista Pittoni the Younger, c.1727–9
Oil on canvas, 2200 × 1390mm
(86⅝ × 54¾")
Fitzwilliam Museum, Cambridge

This elaborate image indicates the European aspect of Newton's fame. Commissioned by an Irish entrepreneur from an Italian artist, it shows figures representing muses and philosophers mourning, and engaging in scholarly discourse with diagrams and instruments as divine light is refracted through a Newtonian prism. His funeral urn fills the niche.

FAR RIGHT **Sir Isaac Newton**
George Bickham, 1732
Engraving, 490 × 310mm
(19¼ × 12¼")
The Wellcome Library, London

This engraving was first published in 1732, and then reissued by the original engraver's son with eulogising verses as Newton's posthumous reputation reached new heights. It commemorates specifically Newton's work on celestial motion. The cherub at top right is misusing his telescope. Newton, 'prince of philosophers', is eternalised as a star.

Sir Isaac Newton
Louis François Roubiliac
Trinity College Chapel, Cambridge

Sir Isaac Newton
David Le Marchand, c.1718
Carved ivory bust, height 240mm (9½")
The British Museum

occasional swindler (he once absconded with the takings of Handel's opera company), undertook probably the most spectacular and international visual promotion of Newton. He commissioned, in Italy, a series of huge allegorical paintings of distinguished Britons, including Robert Boyle (1627–91) and the Duke of Marlborough (1650–1722), aiming to recoup his investment through the sale of engraved copies. In the Newton picture, a prism refracts the divine light shining over Newton's funeral urn. This secular adaptation of the language of religious allegory, with its borrowed sanctity and strong emotional charge, was an effective idiom for building Newton's reputation. We can see it too in cheaper productions, such as the engravings produced by both George Bickhams (d.1758; d.1796), father and son, in 1732 and 1787.

Romantic hero

The portrait bust, with its classical overtones and solemn presence, was an effective way of memorialising Newton, and here, as in the MacSwinny scheme, he usually appeared amongst his fellow Britons; the Frenchman Pierre Grosley (1718–85) noted that both private and public spaces 'were adorned with figures painted and engraved, and with busts of all sizes, made of all sorts of materials, of Bacon, Shakespeare, Milton, Locke, Addison, Newton'. If Rysbrack and Louis François Roubiliac (1705?–62) were kept busy at the top end of the market, mass-production techniques introduced by Josiah Wedgwood (1730–95) – brazenly advertising himself as 'Vase Maker General to the Universe' – and James Tassie (1735–99) ensured a steady supply of portrait medallions.

As the eighteenth century closed, the celebration of Newton as a senior representative of collective rationality was replaced, under the imperative of Romanticism, by a refashioning of him as a one-off genius. As Dr Fara points out, this happened sporadically and without the volume of images and discernible pattern of the eighty or so years immediately after his death. Wordsworth and Blake will be our illustrations. Wordsworth's lines on the Roubiliac full-length statue at Trinity College, Cambridge, put a Romantic spin on a marble intended to convey an impression of a public man engaged in discourse:

> The marble index of a Mind for ever
> Voyaging thro' strange seas of Thought, alone.

'I seem to have been only like a boy playing on the sea-shore and diverting myself in now and then finding a smoother pebble or a prettier shell than ordinary, whilst the great ocean of truth lay all undiscovered before me.' Isaac Newton

William Blake's Newton is something of a monster; his famous print, dated either 1794–5 or 1804–5, depicts a naked, muscular figure called 'Newton', seated on an underwater rock, forcing his recalcitrant paper flat in order to impose upon both it and our perception his rational, geometric view of the world, which was anathema to Blake as the champion of imagination, inspiration and religion. The use of this print by Sir Eduardo Paolozzi as the basis for his statue outside the British Library led to a correspondence in *The Times* in the spring of 1993, in which one side decried the use of an image critical of Newton, while its supporters saw it as an appropriately ambiguous representation, echoing Blake's complexity and current anxieties about the applications of science. There it broods, anyway, conferring on Newton, or perhaps burdening him with, the duty of symbolising the intellectual aspirations of mankind.

We have seen something of the Victorian attitude to Newton when discussing the apple episode – the perceived need to simplify and, in the purest sense, vulgarise Newton and his work. By the 1850s, the image of a simple searcher after truth had been widely disseminated, most concisely through extensive use of the Newton sound bite: 'I seem to have been only like a boy playing on the sea-shore and diverting myself in now and then finding a smoother pebble or a prettier shell than ordinary, whilst the great ocean of truth lay all undiscovered before me.'

In the twentieth century, however, Newton's reputation took some heavy blows. Like all the Great Britons, he suffered from the

Royal Society Gold Medal depicting
Sir Isaac Newton, 1835
Presented to Michael Faraday for his
contributuion to natural knowledge
The Royal Society

Sir Isaac Newton
Salvador Dalí, c.1987
Bronze with black patina
3m 90cm (12' 9")

OPPOSITE
Sir Isaac Newton
Sir Godfrey Kneller, 1702
Oil on canvas
756 × 622mm (29¾ × 24½")
National Portrait Gallery, London (NPG 2881)

loss of Britain's greatness. All idols have feet of clay: those receiving the admiration of our forebears tend now to be viewed more suspiciously, dare we say dispassionately, as men and women with their own agendas, mixed of motivation, frequently causing private grief as well as public benefit. An early blow to Newton's reputation was the emergence of Albert Einstein (1879–1955) before the First World War. Here was a modern, German, Newton: a man with an all-embracing universal theory, and a talent for self-promotion whose exaggerated eccentricities – dislike of socks, wire-wool hair – were 'mad scientist' incarnate. Einstein, like Newton, had powerful disciples and interpreters, prominent among whom in Britain was Bertrand Russell (1872–1970).

Charting the history of science and scientists

Between the wars, the full weight of Soviet scholarship was deployed to deflate Newton's reputation as an individual genius. A Kremlin-briefed heavy mob hijacked the 1931 Congress of the History of Science and Technology held in London, stifling the delegates with the density of their rhetoric. One contribution, however, by Boris Hessen, changed the face of Newton studies and did much to establish the current methodology of the history of science. Hessen placed Newton firmly in his seventeenth-century context, demonstrating that his interests in alchemy, often seen as aberrational, were related to metallurgy and relevant to his work at the Royal Mint, and that his mathematics helped soldiers to aim cannon. (One remembers in this context the delightful 1736 print showing a Newtonian hunter downing two ducks with one shot.) This formidable contribution, Marxist scholarship at its most persuasive in refusing to discuss individual achievement separately from societal developments, exacerbated growing unease with the concept of heroism and left us with a diffuse, even a disembodied, Newton.

Let us conclude with another foreigner's comment on Newton's reputation, that of Salvador Dalí (1904–89). His statue of Newton, conceived around 1970 and executed in bronze in 1987, is explicitly disembodied. The exhibition catalogue (Milan, 1987) explained: 'Dalí shows that the living human being, Sir Isaac Newton, has become a name in science, completely lacking in personality and in individuality, merely a label . . . Therefore, he introduced into the figure two large holes: one removes the viscera and the other the brain . . . Newton the man is gone.' Discuss!

Horatio Nelson

Admiral Lord Nelson, our greatest naval hero,
found public fame not only for his victories
against the Spanish and the French, but also
for his spectacular love affair with Emma,
Lady Hamilton

Horatio Nelson was the most dazzling and successful naval leader and tactician in British history. He won more battles than any other admiral before or since. His startlingly bold style of attack revolutionised naval warfare, and the combination of his victories and his fairness to his men gave the Royal Navy a justified confidence that made the dictum 'Britannia rules the waves' resound for the century following his death at the Battle of Trafalgar in 1805. The blows he dealt Napoleon's navy at the Battle of the Nile in 1798 and at Trafalgar were decisive, and saved Britain from French invasion. These are the facts that form the basis for Nelson's reputation, but alone, they don't explain the worship with which he has been regarded, both during his life and after his death. His myth depends on far more than mastery of the seas.

Nelson's two great qualities as a naval officer were his courage and his humanity. He was a leader so inspirational that when he died, the men of his fleet did 'nothing but Blast their eyes and cry ever since he was killed. God bless you!', as one wrote, continuing, 'Chaps that fought like the devil, sit down and cry like a wench!'

Beloved from his loyal band of captains down to the most junior of cabin boys, his men knew they could rely on him to protect their interests. Discipline was essential to maintain order on board a ship that carried up to 850 men, sometimes for years at a time without leave, and Nelson was no soft touch. Most crucially, though, he recognised that treating his sailors well was the key to a well-run ship. He was always ready with a kind word or a joke to encourage his men, and equally always ready to sacrifice himself for their good and their morale. At the Battle of the Nile, bleeding profusely from a head wound, he was taken down to the sawdust-strewn hospital deck to be sewn up. Nelson refused to be treated before the other injured men, and insisted that the

surgeons not be informed that he needed their attention. Even when he was dying he covered his face and medals with a handkerchief so his men wouldn't see that he had fallen.

Nelson's famous wounds – his missing arm, his blind eye – are the marks of his bravery. In every battle, he led from the front, refusing to contemplate caution or hesitation. A lesser man would have lived for longer. If he had not been hell-bent on achieving the glorious destiny he imagined for himself, and propelled and protected by this determination, his courage might have been foolhardiness. 'I will be a hero', he declared, 'and confiding in Providence, I will brave every danger.' Luckily, Nelson's confidence was as self-fulfilling as it was infectious. 'Westminster Abbey or glorious victory!' he cried at Cape St Vincent, the battle in 1797 that brought him his first taste of fame, when he leapt aboard the Spanish three-decker *San Jose*, sword held triumphantly aloft.

Cape St Vincent was where Nelson's talent for self-promotion came to the fore, too. A commodore, not yet commander of the fleet, he acted on his own initiative, and thus secured victory. Perhaps because of this disregard for orders, Admiral Jervis (1735–1823) did not mention Nelson's action in his report back to London, but Nelson took it upon himself to write home, describing 'Nelson's Patent Bridge for Boarding First-Rates' (using one enemy ship as a bridge to board and take another) and authorising his friend to send this unofficial account to the newspapers. The myth-making had begun.

In his very weaknesses lay Nelson's strengths. He was considered such a liability by the Admiralty that they never made him a full admiral. His propensity to follow his own instincts rather than obey orders, his desire for personal celebrity, and his public extramarital passion for Emma Hamilton (1765–1815) shocked the traditionalists under whom he served, but made him the man he was. Nelson was

Horatio Nelson 1758–1805

29 September 1758 — Born at Burnham Thorpe, Norfolk, to Revd Edmund Nelson and his wife Catherine. He remains deeply religious throughout his life

1770 — Joins the 64-gun ship *Raisonnable* following an offer of help from his uncle

June 1779 — Nelson rises rapidly through the navy and is appointed captain of the *Hinchinbroke*

March 1787 — Nelson marries Frances Nisbet at Nevis, in the Caribbean. He is put on half pay for the next five years and becomes frustrated at not being in service

21 January 1793 — Execution of King Louis XVI of France. Nelson is appointed to command the *Agamemnon* and sails to the Mediterranean where he visits Naples and meets the Hamiltons

July 1794 — Nelson's right eye is injured at the battle of Calvi during the Corsica campaign

1797 — Nelson is created Rear-Admiral of the Blue but in July he loses his right arm during an attack on Santa Cruz, Tenerife

1798 — Battle of the Nile: Nelson successfully attacks Napoleon's fleet in Aboukir Bay. He spends time in Naples with Lady Hamilton

1801 — Promoted to Vice-Admiral, Nelson's fearless command is shown at the Battle of Copenhagen when he ignores orders to cease action by claiming that he could not see the signal. Nelson's mistress, Emma Hamilton, gives birth to Horatia

May 1803 — Britain declares war on France and Nelson is appointed Commander-in-Chief of the Mediterranean Fleet

1804 — Nelson blockades the French Mediterranean ports and on 14 December Spain declares war on Britain

21 October 1805 — Nelson is killed at the Battle of Trafalgar after destroying the combined French and Spanish fleets. His funeral is held in January 1806 at St Paul's Cathedral

a maverick genius, impulsive and emotional, and the old guard disapproved of him only slightly less than they needed him.

The public, however, loved him unreservedly, more for his flaws than despite them. Had he not been notorious for his affair with the flamboyant Lady Hamilton, had he not paraded through Britain – usually with Emma and her husband, Sir William Hamilton (1730–1803) – as an instantly recognisable figure, with his empty jacket arm pinned to his chest below his diamond decorations, revelling in the attention and adoration he received, and had he not stepped eagerly, gloriously, into the role of national hero, he would not have been the Nelson we still revere. Without his faults and frailties, we would remember him today as a brilliant commander, yes – but not as a hero, Britain's first and greatest, who became the prototype for all our heroes to come.

Laurence Olivier (1907–89) and Vivien Leigh (1913–67) in *Lady Hamilton*, 1941

Although too beautiful – and too young – Laurence Olivier and Vivien Leigh's incarnation of Nelson and Emma Hamilton has helped fuel their enduring myth.

The image of a war-hero

'The death of Nelson was felt in England as something more than a public calamity; men started at the intelligence, and turned pale, as if they had heard of the loss of a dear friend.'

ROBERT SOUTHEY (1774–1843), *The Life of Nelson* (1813)

Horatio Nelson, Viscount Nelson
Sir William Beechey, 1800
Oil on canvas, 623 × 483mm (24½ × 19")
National Portrait Gallery, London (NPG 5798)

This vivid sketch was for the portrait commissioned from Beechey by the City of Norwich. It shows Nelson with brown rather than blue eyes. Nelson gladly accepted numerous British and foreign decorations. Wearing a selection of them on the quarterdeck of the *Victory* at the Battle of Trafalgar, he was a conspicuous target.

Captain Polson of the 60th Foot, the Duke of Clarence (1765–1837), and the austere, stately Lady Lavinia Spencer (d.1831) all had similar reactions on meeting Horatio Nelson for the first time: Polson, about to undertake a dangerous amphibious assault, wondered why the navy had sent him a 'light-haired boy' of 'little account'; Clarence, later William IV, encountered a strange, quaint-looking boy dressed as a captain and 'had never seen anything like it before'; Lady Lavinia quivered with aristocratic disdain, 'a most uncouth creature . . . his general appearance was that of an idiot . . .', but she continued, in words echoing the experience of the two men, 'when he spoke and his wonderful mind broke forth, it was a sort of surprise that riveted my whole attention.'

The qualities of leadership

He surprises us and intrigues us still with his transparent humanity; fine qualities co-existed with petulance, irritability, vanity, self-aggrandisement and insubordination, in a man 'who doesn't understand any language but his own', as Sir William Hamilton remarked. His spectacular and protracted cuckolding of Sir William, the passionate thraldom in which Emma Hamilton held him and the public reaction to their ostentatious affair, all afford us an insight into human behaviour rarely granted by those after whom we name towns, streets, and pubs. Nelson's life contains more layers of complexity, more contrasting textures, more quirks and idiosyncrasies of character, more laughter and groans, than in any work of fiction. Here is a human hero, a popular hero, the first Briton to be a national hero in his own lifetime, even before his dramatic death enshrined him.

We remember him because he made sure that the material was there. An undersized boy from a poor clergyman's large family, after the early loss of an influential uncle he learned that high distinction

Horatio Nelson, Viscount Nelson
John Rigaud, 1781
Oil on canvas, 1270 × 1015mm (50 × 40″)
National Maritime Museum, London

Painted for Captain Locker, this portrait was begun
in 1779 when Nelson was a lieutenant and finished
in 1781 when he was a captain. Locker became
Nelson's mentor and inspired the directness of
attack that became Nelson's naval hallmark, the
tactical boldness of which the ultimate expression
was the breaking of the French line at Trafalgar
(1805). Such courageous methods ensured Nelson
rapid promotion in wartime, although he had no
command from November 1787 to January 1793.

could only be achieved by his own efforts, but also that these endeavours
should be brought clearly to people's notice. He wrote self-promoting
letters to influential public figures, articles for newspapers and self-
praising despatches; he gave interviews to biographers and made
numerous public appearances. He was angry when higher-ranking
officers gave him scant praise: 'I was the mover of it – I was the cause of
its success,' he wrote angrily after the taking of Bastia in 1794. He was
usually right, and knew he was, and this utter confidence could lead
to what we might call creative insubordination, which he characterised
with masterly self-enhancement as 'the Nelson Touch'. This maverick
spirit is the core of much of his memorability: he took his ship out of
line at the Battle of Cape St Vincent to attack the Spaniards; he 'did
not see the signal' at the Battle of Copenhagen (1801); at the Battle of
the Nile, he broke several rules by attacking after dark, in uncharted
water. A failed maverick is an insubordinate liability; a successful
and communicative one is a bold and remembered innovator.

The Hero of the Nile
James Gillray, published 1 December, 1798
Hand-coloured etching, 346 × 236mm (13⅝ × 9¼″)
National Portrait Gallery, London (NPG D12668)

In this cartoon Gillray mocks Nelson's vanity. Despite his exhaustion after the battle, Nelson remains weighed down by a scarlet cloak and the *chelengk* on his hat, both awarded to him by the Sultan of Turkey. Money bags appear in his coat of arms.

'Well then, I exclaimed, I will be a hero, and confiding in Providence I will brave every danger.'
Horatio Nelson, 'Sketch of My Life'

Nelson craved distinction; he did not have the aristocrat's understated sense of national duty, the inborn belief that the privileges of high social rank are paid for through service. The war with France created a need to expand the elite officer class, to co-opt into it professional talent, both to win the war and to protect the officer's privileges from the revolutionary French and their potential allies among the more aggressive elements of British radicalism. Decorations and titles were the glittering prizes, for which parvenu sea officers competed vigorously, and none more so than Nelson. He went for them as he went for the French, unequivocally, directly and unashamedly: 'A peerage or Westminster Abbey!' he intoned before the battle of the Nile, echoing his earlier cry at Cape St Vincent. It sounds irredeemably corny, but for him it was a personal manifesto.

That sound bite was a distillation of the explanation of the defining moment of his life that Nelson gave a few years later in 'Sketch of My Life', written for his biographers James Clarke (1765?–1834) and John McArthur (1755–1840). Recovering from a bout of fever on a voyage home, the eighteen-year-old Nelson's depressed mood was transformed by a vision of a 'radiant orb'. 'A sudden glow of patriotism was kindled within me and presented my king and my country as my patron. Well then, I exclaimed, I will be a hero, and confiding in Providence I will brave every danger.' That was how he chose to record his motivation for posterity, with, as the historian Linda Colley has written, euphoric bravery and beguiling egotism; the sceptic may discern a degree of retrospective reputation-fashioning, but it certainly illuminates the pattern of his life and death.

Conspicuous personal sacrifice

To be memorable, our picture of the past requires clear narrative structure, piquant incident and emotional colour to give it durability. Nelson provided all this, with both the events themselves and his own interpretation of them. The spine of his narrative is made up of the three great set-piece battles of Cape St Vincent, the Nile and Copenhagen, each of which brought him higher public distinction and popular acclaim expressed in a mass of two- and three-dimensional visual material. The regular wounds, too, form part of the narrative pattern, each one a bloody reminder of his vulnerability, and his empty sleeve became as effective a short-cut to identification as Churchill's cigar or Chaplin's cane. Then came Trafalgar and the death he had always

ABOVE **Death of Admiral Lord Nelson**
Arthur William Devis, 1807
Oil on canvas, 623 × 483mm (24½ × 19″)
National Maritime Museum, London

RIGHT **The Death of Wolfe**
William Woollett after Benjamin West, published 1776
Engraving, 428 × 593mm (16⅞ × 23⅜″)
National Portrait Gallery, London (NPG D1356)

Nelson's hero was Major-General James Wolfe, who died during
an attack on Quebec in 1759. Benjamin West's *The Death of Wolfe*
(1771) planted a fruitful seed and Nelson asked West to record
his own death similarly, should he be killed in battle. Paintings of
death in battle became powerful and patriotic commemorators
of the sacrifice demanded in pursuit of victory. Highly dramatic,
they drew on the art-historical conventions of both Christian and
mythological art, substituting modern naval and military uniforms
for togas and tunics, and sublimating spiritual fervour and classical
stoicism into a quasi-religious British nationalism. Nelson's death
at the height of the Battle of Trafalgar was the subject of numerous
paintings in this genre, from Devis's illustrated here to those of
Daniel Maclise and Benjamin West himself, both held by the
Walker Art Gallery, Liverpool.

Horatio Nelson, Viscount Nelson
Guy Head, 1798–9
Oil on canvas, 2229 × 1689mm (87¾ × 66½")
National Portrait Gallery, London (NPG 5101)

Selection of commemorative ceramics
National Maritime Museum, London

accepted as a professional risk, the likely result of the style of leadership demanded by naval warfare. Nelson had imagination, and a sense of the dramatic potential of conspicuous personal sacrifice, and to some extent could even be said to have sketched out the scenario of his own posthumous depiction. Shortly before his death, he had met Benjamin West (1728–1820), the President of the Royal Academy, and having said how much he admired that painter's celebrated *The Death of Wolfe*, asked why he had made no more such paintings. West replied that there had been no suitable subjects recently, and then added, 'My Lord, I fear your intrepidity may yet furnish me with another such scene, and if it should, I should certainly avail myself of it.' Nelson replied, '*Will* you, Mr West? Then I hope I shall die in the next battle.'

Documentary painting

West did his duty, but in attempting excessive incidental detail, he failed to reproduce the intensity of his painting of General Wolfe. The most haunting and resonant image, produced by Arthur Devis (1712–87), now hangs in the National Maritime Museum at Greenwich. Devis researched it thoroughly, visiting Nelson's flagship, the *Victory*, on her return to Portsmouth, and spending three weeks sketching and interviewing those present at Nelson's death, persuading them to pose. Compared with most paintings of the genre, it is a model of documentary accuracy: although Devis increased the headroom of the cockpit for pictorial effect and included some characters who were not actually present, details such as the chaplain, Dr Scott, rubbing the dying Admiral's chest are authentic. Its power, though, is contained in the allusions, which transform it into an icon of national sacrifice. Devis shifts the emotion from that of the particular event to generalised Christian notions of selfless sacrifice, and the Christian iconography is everywhere: Nelson's everyday uniform has been replaced by a loose sheet; he is haloed by a lamp hanging from above; the great beams intersect in the shape of the true cross, imbuing with religious significance the wooden deck of the ship from which his near-dead body has been taken down; and his disciples crowd around in grief.

Linda Colley reminds us that such images, reproduced in affordable media, had a tremendous contemporary impact, not only on the ordinary people who bought cut-outs, prints and cheap crockery

RIGHT **Horatio Nelson, Viscount Nelson**
Lemuel Francis Abbott, 1797
Oil on canvas, 749 × 622mm (29½ × 24¼")
National Portrait Gallery, London (NPG 394)

BELOW LEFT **The Nelson Pillar, Dublin** (detail)
George Petrie after R. Winkles, published 1829
Engraving, 1960 × 1410mm (77⅛ × 55½")
National Maritime Museum, London

Similar in design to the monument in Trafalgar
Square, the pillar was erected in 1806 in
Sackville Street, and stood until 1966 when
destroyed during the troubles.

BELOW RIGHT **Funeral Procession of
the Late Lord Nelson** (detail)
John Hill after Augustus Charles Pugin,
published 1 April 1806
Coloured aquatint, 400 × 500mm (15¾ × 19¾")
National Maritime Museum, London

The *Victory* brought Nelson's coffin to
Greenwich. It was then taken by admiral's barge
to Whitehall Stairs. The next morning, 9 January
1806, thirty-two admirals and over 100 captains
escorted him to St Paul's. So quiet were the
crowds that the rustling of doffed hats was like
a murmuring sea.

adorned with the scenes, but also on the elite themselves, who saw their courage and resolution depicted in a contemporary setting, that also reflected the stoicism and sacrifice for high principles of the classical and Christian models they so admired. And what do we make of such scenes? The emotion, the assertive patriotism, the hijacking of religious iconography for nationalistic ends, the glorification of war – all mawkish, exaggerated, embarrassing, inappropriate? Evasive as it may sound, it depends on who you mean by 'we', and on whether you approach such art as conveying messages for ourselves today, or whether you agree with the novelist L. P. Hartley (1895–1972), who famously wrote, 'The past is a foreign country: they do things differently there.'

Nelson claimed to have little discrimination in artistic matters, because of a restricted education, but he certainly appreciated the celebratory and commemorative function of public art, and the simultaneously public and private nature of portraiture. Professional pride, social insecurity and vanity all contributed to, as Admiral Lord St Vincent (previously Admiral Jervis) commented, Nelson 'sitting to every painter in London', and this enthusiasm forms part of an assertive public display judged offensive by many of his superior officers and the *bon ton* of late-Georgian society. In his defence, it should be pointed out that two of the earliest portraits, by John Francis Rigaud (1742–1810) and Lemuel Francis Abbott (c.1760–1803), were commissioned by Nelson's mentor Captain William Locker

Dido in Despair
James Gillray, published 6 February 1801
Hand-coloured etching and stipple engraving,
266 × 376mm (10½ × 14¾")
National Portrait Gallery, London (NPG D13034)

This mockery of Emma Hamilton's classical 'attitudes' was produced as Nelson left England before the Battle of Copenhagen (1801). Emma is fat and blowsy, lamenting her hero's departure as Sir William sleeps. Emma was trying to conceal her pregnancy, to which Sir William, ever the gentleman, was the first in the household to turn a blind eye. The title refers to the desertion of Dido, Queen of Carthage, by her lover, Aeneas.

Emma, Lady Hamilton (1765–1815)
George Romney, c.1782–6
Oil on canvas, 622 × 546mm (24½ × 21½")
National Portrait Gallery, London (NPG 4448)

'Emma is looking out for the softest pillows to repose the few wearied limbs you have left', said her husband Sir William Hamilton to Nelson, when the battered Admiral arrived in Naples in 1798, after the Battle of the Nile. As Emma hero-worshipped Nelson and nursed him back to health, they fell in love. Many patrician observers, both in Naples and after the lovers returned to Britain, found their unconventional social behaviour brash and unacceptable, and their contrasting sizes ridiculous. Posterity has been a kinder judge, relishing the human vulnerability of the courageous Admiral and the indomitable spirit of his lover.

(1731–1800), and others were commissioned by admirers, not least among whom was Emma Hamilton.

Conspicuous in his portraits, as in his public appearances, were the British and foreign decorations showered upon him, notoriously the spinning clockwork *chelengk* awarded him by the Sultan of Turkey; as the caricaturist James Gillray (1757–1815) demonstrated, this was taken to the point of contemporary parody. To his chagrin, he received a relatively minor ennoblement after the Battle of the Nile, which was not, he thought, sufficient recognition of his achievement. In this resentment he may have been influenced by Emma Hamilton who said, in her *fortissimo* way, that he should be 'DUKE NELSON MARQUIS NILE EARL ALEXANDER VICOUNT [sic] PYRAMID BARON CROCADILE [sic] AND PRINCE VICTORY'. Emma also was a social climber, making her way up from kept woman to wife of an aristocrat and intimate friend of the Queen of Naples. She was determined that her Horatio should receive his due, and she too put a high value on portraits of him, having herself kept artists, particularly George Romney (1734–1802), busy since the early 1780s.

A notorious romantic

Nelson's relationship with Emma Hamilton, the acceptance of it by her husband Sir William, and the public reaction to the whole phenomenon have been a steady guarantee of enduring notoriety. This is a live issue still, because we have not resolved whether or not a 'great' person may retain that accolade if they are, by conventional, Christian moral standards, a sinner. Nowadays, some people appear still to be uneasy about the relationship between unconventional sexual behaviour and the holding of public office or the receiving of honours. There are those who resent revisionist interpretations of the personalities of history as some kind of betrayal of trust, seeing them as disloyal mud-slinging. Nelson's case is a very good example of how a balanced interpretation of a famous person, which allows human faults to be exposed, does not in the least diminish admiration and celebration of his professional brilliance and personal charm. Our history – and in many ways this is a very positive development – is now for our entertainment as much as for our edification: we are not building an empire or fighting a conventional war, and we no longer need mythical leaders as role models. We can enjoy a good story for its own sake, particularly if the characters, like Nelson and

Arthur Wellesley, 1st Duke of Wellington
(1769–1852)
Robert Home, 1804
Oil on canvas, 749 × 622mm (29½ × 24½")
National Portrait Gallery, London (NPG 1471)

This painting depicts Wellington as the victorious
Commander in India, before his return in 1805.
Wellington's understated patrician style contrasted
with Nelson's pushiness. They met once: after initial
suspicion, Wellington approved of Nelson's wise
appreciation of the international situation.

OPPOSITE
Horatio Nelson, Viscount Nelson
Lemuel Francis Abbott, 1800
Oil on canvas, 762 × 635mm (30 × 25")
National Maritime Museum, London

This is a later version of the painting by Abbott
illustrated earlier on page 91. On the earlier version
Nelson proudly wore the Order of the Bath, awarded
after the Battle of Cape St Vincent in 1797. Now the
Bath jostles with a plethora of foreign orders, the
rewards of the Battle of the Nile.

Lady Hamilton, are so spectacular that we can accept them as players
in a vast, colourful, popular drama. And if we are to be educated, let it
be to a greater understanding of human diversity.

Contemporary heroes

Nelson's reputation as the finest sea officer of his age is unassailable.
It is intriguing that the Duke of Wellington (1769–1852), the British
Army's most successful commander, who was making his reputation
in India during Nelson's last years, was such a complete contrast.
Wellington was a reserved patrician, moving easily in the highest
society, deeply suspicious of popular acclaim, and although sharing
with Nelson the misery of an unhappy marriage, measured and
discreet in his compensatory affairs. Wellington's style, evinced in his
plain dress and attitude to titles, to which he was openly indifferent,
could not be further from Nelson's. His biographer Elizabeth Longford
had the measure of both men: 'Sensitivity to the responses of others
could produce, as in Nelson, both a unique grace of leadership and
the weakness of vanity. Neither that particular grace nor that failing
were among Wellington's endowments.'

Several Great Britons have modern organisations dedicated to
the commemoration and perpetuation of their achievements: the
William Blake Society, the Dickens Fellowship, the Jane Austen
Society and the Cromwell Association, amongst others. Both the
Nelson Society (including its junior section, the Topsail Group) and
the 1805 Club are devoted to his memory and offer a wide-ranging and
vigorous programme of public events, activities and publications. Much
of this is now focused on the 'Nelson Decade', the rolling programme
of bicentennial commemorations, which will culminate on Trafalgar
Day, 21 October, in 2005. HMS *Victory*, the Royal Naval Museum at
Portsmouth, the National Maritime Museum at Greenwich and the
Nelson Museum at Monmouth are wholly or partly dedicated to his
memory, and to the traditions he has come to represent. If you want
to study Nelson at home, there are over 1,000 books to read, including
Barry Unsworth's intriguing novel *Losing Nelson*, as well as numerous
websites, while on television you are bound to catch one of the twenty
or so films and documentaries in which he features, sometimes
appearing more handsome, in the form of Laurence Olivier (1907–89)
or Peter Finch (1916–77), than even Sir William Beechey (1753–1839) or
John Hoppner (1758–1810) was ever able to make him.

Isambard Kingdom Brunel

The most talented and original engineer of
his generation, Brunel transformed Britain's
industrial landscape with his ambitious
designs for railways, ships and bridges

'The most prolific and talented engineer and innovator of them all – Isambard Kingdom Brunel'

Jeremy Clarkson, writer and presenter

So, what made Britain great? Well, it certainly wasn't music or art. It wasn't royalty, most of whom seem to have spent their time cutting people's heads off. And nor was it William Shakespeare who, so far as I'm concerned, did nothing but bring four hundred years of misery to the school classroom.

No, what made Britain great, what put this tiny country on the map and turned the world pink, was our innovators and our engineers. They powered the Industrial Revolution, and built the ships and won the wars. They invented the medicines and developed communication. Thomas Telford, James Watt, George Stephenson, James Brindley, Alexander Fleming, the list is endless. If it was invented, it was invented here.

And sitting right at the top of the pile has to be the most prolific and talented engineer and innovator of them all – Isambard Kingdom Brunel.

Brunel was not terribly interested in personal fortune. In his entire life, he didn't take out a single patent, saying that such things stifled competition and held back advancement. Furthermore, if it came to a choice between making money and 'getting the job done', the job would always win. Time and again, he refused to take payment for work and, if he felt shareholders needed a prod, he'd invest his own money in a scheme, just to show how much faith he had in it.

Yes, he had an ego. Yes, he was fuelled by the adoration of a grateful nation. But the nation had every right to be grateful, because Brunel started mankind on its headlong rush into the technological age.

Darwin told us where we had come from. Brunel took us to where we were going. Really. If it can be argued that Britain built the modern world, and that Brunel built modern Britain, then it stands to reason that Brunel built the modern world. And that makes him pretty damn great in my book.

For most people, Isambard Kingdom Brunel – and he should win this contest for his name alone – is best remembered for the Clifton Suspension Bridge in Bristol. Which is strange because this is about the only piece of nineteenth-century architecture for which he was arguably not responsible. (Yes, he came up with the idea, and even referred to the project tenderly as my 'first child, my darling', but endless problems with money meant it was not completed until after his death.)

There's no doubt he could have pushed harder, but unfortunately he was a little bit busy. To start with, he worked on building a tunnel under the Thames – the first tunnel ever to run under a body of water – and then, when this apprenticeship was over, he was off . . .

His name is all over the Great Western Railway from London to Bristol, along with a number of other railways in the South of England, Italy and India. Then there was the Hungerford footbridge over the Thames and the Royal Albert Bridge over the Tamar in Cornwall. (In fact, let's not get bogged down with his bridges, because it would take us too long.)

We could talk at this point about his railway tunnel at Box in Wiltshire, which, at two miles long, was the longest in the world at the time. We could mention the fact that it was unlined, something thought to be geologically impossible. But we've done tunnels.

So let's move on to his ships. He designed the SS *Great Western*, the first steamship ever to cross the Atlantic, and the SS *Great Britain*, the first ocean-going liner ever to have an iron hull, and the first to be driven by a propeller.

Then there was the *Great Eastern*, the biggest ship the world had ever seen (and, moreover, the biggest ship it would see until the *Lusitania* came along nearly half a century later). It was the *Great Eastern* that laid the first

Isambard Kingdom Brunel 1806–59

Atlantic telegraph cable connecting Britain to America. Shakespeare's Puck may have said he'd put a girdle around the world, but Brunel actually did it.

In between times, he amused himself by designing a few harbours, some sea walls, the floating docks in Bristol, and an observatory or two. It was Brunel who invented rifling down the inside of a gun's barrel, and Brunel who designed a portable field hospital for Florence Nightingale (1820–1910). And let's not forget his iceberg warning device, a tube that carried water from the front of the ship to a thermometer on the bridge. Simple. Effective. (And unfortunately not fitted to the *Titanic*.)

Then there were his buildings. Perhaps the most famous is Paddington Station, which was modelled on the Crystal Palace, home of the Great Exhibition in 1851.

I go through Paddington whenever I come to London by train, but not until I started work on making the *Great Britons* programme did I ever pause to take in its extraordinary majesty. The moons and the stars cut into the beams, the

iron pillars that double as drainage points for that huge glass roof. Next time you're there, take a break from poring over the departure board, and look up. It's quite a spectacle.

Furthermore, Brunel's designs weren't just aesthetically beautiful – and they were beautiful: the bridge over the Thames at Maidenhead is an exquisite example – but they were also strong. Too strong, perhaps. It's hard to think of anything built today that will last a hundred years. Engineers and architects nowadays are keeping their professions going with an endless succession of designs that need to be replaced every fifteen minutes. Brunel, however, didn't think like that. He really wanted his pieces to last for a century, and they have done. Which means that, in his own small, inadvertent way, Brunel actually helped kill off the engineering profession in Britain. By the time he was finished, there was nothing left for anyone else to do.

If we had continued at the furious pace that Brunel set, we would now be fighting one another with light-sabres. *Bladerunner* would be a vision of the past.

The image of an engineer

'[a] man with the greatest originality of thought and
power of execution, bold in his plans but right.'

DANIEL GOOCH (1816–89)

Isambard Kingdom Brunel
Horrace Harral, after a photograph by
Robert Howlett
Engraving, published 1858
National Portrait Gallery, London (NPG D1127)

It is one of the great portraits. A small man in a big hat, hands
awkward in the high-cut pockets of his muddy trousers, cigar gripped
in a chain-smoker's lip-end clamp, his casual yet commanding stance
echoing those of earlier pioneers like Drake or Ralegh, or a general
in his warlike element painted by Sir Joshua Reynolds (1723–92).
Behind him hang the massive chains, crowding him, elbowing into
the picture space, competing for the attention due to them as symbols
of the man, his ambitions and the age he bestrode. In another
photograph – taken, one presumes, within the duration of the same
cigar – the camera has been turned to the right to include the curve
of the great drum that holds the chains. The foreground is cluttered,
and Brunel has altered his pose: he leans on the chains, as one
commentator recently said, 'like a yob at a bus stop'. The magic
has gone. In yet another image he sits on the block, looking lumpy
and tired, oppressed rather than commanding. Brunel, as far as we
know, and as these photographs bear out, was indifferent to his
image. The fact that we have pictures of him at all is due not to his
interest or efforts, but entirely to those of others.

Shot on location

The sequence of photographs to which this belongs, and which was
taken by Robert Howlett (1830–58) for a feature published in the
Illustrated Times on 16 January 1858, is a valuable record of the first
attempt to launch the *Great Eastern* into the Thames at Napier Yard,
Millwall, on 3 November 1857. Howlett's brief was to record the event
and the key personalities, in a series of photographs that were copied
and printed as engravings, as the direct printing of photographs was
not then possible. He was a skilful photographer with an eye for a
striking setting, as the use of the chains shows, and perhaps he was
also the one to persuade the busy and anxious engineer to pose for
a number of shots. With one of them, Howlett struck gold; it was the

CLOCKWISE FROM TOP LEFT

Isambard Kingdom Brunel

All by Robert Howlett, 1857

Albumen print, 286 × 225mm (11¼ × 8⅞")
National Portrait Gallery, London (NPG P112)

Albumen print, 270 × 216mm (10⅝ × 8½")
National Portrait Gallery, London (NPG P662)

Robert Howlett and Georges Downes, 1857
Stereoscopic photographs, 168 × 80mm (6½ × 3⅛")

The photograph of Brunel standing in front of the chains of the SS *Great Eastern* captures the spirit and modernity of Victorian engineering. The photograph was taken as the basis for an engraving to celebrate the launch of the steamship in the *Illustrated Times*. Howlett's series of images illustrates the power of the medium to evoke a personality and a place in time. The series also demonstrates the power of picture editing, for amongst all the shots taken by Howlett there is only one photograph with the power to have fixed Brunel – with his hat, cigar, fob-watch and dirty boots – in the public's mind.

Robert Stephenson (1803–59)
John Lucas
Oil on canvas, 763 × 601mm (30 × 23⅝")
National Portrait Gallery, London (NPG 5792)

Robert Stephenson, the son of George, supervised
the building of the Rocket locomotive before
becoming engineer for the London to Birmingham
line. He and Brunel were rivals and they argued over
the railway gauge, with Brunel believing – probably
rightly – that a broader gauge would give stability and
allow trains to travel faster. The battle was eventually
fought in Parliament, where Brunel lost his argument,
because by then there were 1,900 miles of narrow-
gauge and only 274 miles of broad-gauge track.

Robert Stephenson (1803–59) with the great
hydraulic ram used in launching the *Leviathan*
Horace Harral, after a photograph by Robert
Howlett, c. 1858
Wood engraving, 174 × 231mm (6⅞ × 9⅛")
National Portrait Gallery, London (NPG D6865)

This engraving of Robert Stephenson can be
compared with that of Brunel on page 100, which
was commissioned for the same newspaper.

obvious choice to reproduce, and in our own age, dominated as
it is by the manipulative presentation of public figures, this image
resonates with the simplicity of genius.

Also present at Millwall on that dull November day was Brunel's
rival and friend Robert Stephenson (1803–59), the mechanical and
structural engineer and son of the celebrated George Stephenson
(1781–1848). Robert Stephenson was a brilliant engineer, the most
significant developer of the railway locomotive, and builder of both
the ingenious tubular Britannia Bridge over the Menai Straits and the
sublime curve of the Royal Border Bridge at Berwick. Although much
respected by his professional successors and historians, in popular
memory his reputation has suffered by being merged with his
father's. Furthermore, Robert was a steady, cautious, unflamboyant
operator, prosaically named compared to Brunel, and unremarkably
portrayed. The surviving images of Robert, and of George, are
conventional, worthy rather than exciting, and give little sense of
the revolutionary drama of industrial pioneering.

Building bridges

Robert was present at Millwall in response to a plea for help from
Brunel. 'It was very delightful,' wrote Brunel in 1846, 'in the midst of
our incessant personal professional contests, carried to the extreme
limit of fair opposition, to meet him on a perfectly friendly footing
and discuss engineering points.' The friendship between the two
great professional rivals, diametrically opposed to each other tempera-
mentally and in their approach to engineering problems, was sincere.
Brunel had previously dropped all his engagements in 1849 to help
Stephenson and other engineers with the Britannia Bridge, and now
Stephenson, ill and tired as he was, returned the compliment.

Howlett's image of Brunel combines the man and the work with
simple eloquence, conveying vitality, quirkiness and the dirt of
endeavour with all the raw directness of an early photograph, and
providing enough narrative leads to satisfy the most ardent post-
modern deconstructor. It is this synergy that gives the image its
power. Few other photographs have by themselves contributed so
much to the perpetuation of a reputation. Most photographs of
Victorian celebrities are studio-bound; those of Florence Nightingale,
for instance, post-date her pioneering nursing work in the Crimea,
and lack the immediacy and truth of the Brunel image, placed firmly

Conference of Engineers at the Menai Straits
James Scott after John Lucas, published 1868
Mezzotint print, 549 × 720mm (21⅝ × 28⅜")
National Portrait Gallery, London (NPG D10713)

Engineering was a high-risk profession in the mid-nineteenth century, but both its status and public interest increased with the creation of vast new buildings and structures. This mezzotint captures a series of better-known figures (including Latimer Clark (1822–98), Edwin Clark (1814–94), Frank Forster (1800–52), George Parker Bidder (1806–78), Robert Stephenson, Joseph Locke (1805–60) and Isambard Kingdom Brunel) preparing to float one of the tubes of the Britannia Bridge. Such prints were popular in demonstrating the work of engineers to a broad audience. This one celebrates the co-operative spirit that persisted, despite commercial rivalry.

Brunel University
Founded as a college in Middlesex in the 1920s to provide recruits for local industry, Brunel University now takes in over 12,000 students and an international contingent drawn from 91 countries.

in an actual moment of historical time. This Brunel stirs the imagination: he evokes the clanging cacophony of the shipyard, the slapping of the Thames on the slipways, the towering of the great hull above the terraced houses and riverside flatlands.

Heroic feats

The photograph captures the engineer as hero: the man with the vision to harness the motive power of steam to shrink the world. Brunel saw not merely Bristol at the end of the line, but New York across the western ocean; not just a big ship to go to the New World, but the biggest ever constructed, powered by both propellers and paddle-wheels, with auxiliary sails, and carrying enough coal for the entire return journey to Australia. He stretched engineering and construction technology beyond the limits of possibility, and failures and disasters occurred at regular intervals, yet he was indomitable and indefatigable. He was not immortal, though: he sacrificed his bodily health and peace of mind to his drive and ambition. The *Great Eastern* project destroyed him. In the photograph we see the jaunty, confident engineer: two years later, the problems having multiplied, he was, according to his biographer L. T. C. Rolt (1910–74), 'scarcely recognisable in this shrunken, pitiful figure that moved with painful difficulty about the decks with the support of a

Isambard Kingdom Brunel
D. J. Pound, after a photograph by
John Mayall, published 1859
Engraving, 287 × 207mm (11¼ × 8⅛")
National Portrait Gallery, London (NPG D1126)

Both this engraving and the painting of Brunel on
page 107 are unfamiliar representations. They were
commissioned when Brunel was at the height of his
engineering fame (the painting is by his brother-in-
law John Callcott Horsley), but there are few signs of
his power, profession or character. Brunel is reported
to have been a workaholic who would readily work
an eighteen-hour day and sleep in his office. His
honeymoon allegedly consisted of three days in
Capel Curig in North Wales and included a visit to
the Liverpool–Manchester railway.

OPPOSITE
Isambard Kingdom Brunel
with (left to right) the harbour master,
Lord Carlisle, Lord Paget and Mr Yates
Robert Howlett and George Downs, c.1857
Sepia albumen print, 204 × 160mm (8 × 6¼")
National Portrait Gallery, London (RN 25078)

stick . . . the mass of dark hair had receded from the high forehead, the full face had fallen in and the mouth had pursed to a straight, thin-lipped line of pain. There were dropsical bags under the dark eyes, but the eyes themselves had become a redoubt where the forces of life were fighting their last stubborn rearguard action.'

Brunel died on the *Great Eastern* as surely as Nelson died on the quarterdeck of the *Victory*. We can perhaps, without being over-fanciful, sense the oppressive, threatening weight of the chains, pressing on to the tiny figure of their creator and overwhelming him. The story of the building, launch and maiden voyage of the great ship has the grandeur, inexorability and universality of great tragedy. The vibrant hero, his greatest project on the verge of disaster because of the chicanery and incompetence of lesser men, drives on relent-lessly, overcoming technical and financial difficulties, only for even greater ones to present themselves. Eventually, his great ship is ready to sail on her maiden voyage, but Brunel collapses with a stroke and is carried down her side and back to his house in Duke Street. Gravely ill, he waits for reports of the first journey. When news comes, it is of disaster: an explosion, caused by steam stopcocks being left closed, has blown off a funnel and killed several crew members. Broken finally in spirit, Brunel died a week later, on 15 September 1859.

Noble sacrifice

How do we, in a society less at ease with self-denial, view this self-sacrifice? It is easier to understand the death of Nelson, accepting the risk of his inherently dangerous profession, dying within his hazardous element. After all, we still expect our armed forces to take that risk. What is awesome and, to us, disturbing about Brunel, and to some extent his friend Robert Stephenson, was the willingness to give body and soul to a job, to the detriment of physical and mental health.

What about the stress, we ask? How did they cope? We revisit their stories with a sense of awe and wonder, appalled, yet fascinated by such total, self-destructive commitment. We seek to understand the complex motivation behind such actions. We note with interest that his biographer has identified a core of melancholy, that the engine of the astonishing man was nervous energy driving him to overcome feelings of doubt, despair and pessimism. That, we think, is more like it! A modern, post-Freudian explanation, in tune with

our self-absorbed awareness of human frailty and complexity. So we reassess the achievers of the past in the light of our society's concerns. Such revisionism, if undertaken in a magnanimous spirit of enquiry, celebrating human difference and with a due recognition that we merely add our generation's ideas to a permanent debate, is a positive contribution.

Executive power

Our interest in and understanding of human motivation makes us suspicious of leaders: what's in it for them, we ask? By what devious means are they trying to win us over to do their bidding? Few heads of enterprises have led so conspicuously as Brunel. He insisted on full responsibility for any project, and ran things with absolute, but humane, authority. He chose his subordinates carefully, trusted them utterly, and defended them against interference from other senior staff and directors. If they defaulted, he was merciless: 'Plain, gentlemanly language seems to have no effect upon you. I must try stronger language and stronger measures. You are a cursed, lazy, inattentive, apathetic vagabond . . . you have wasted more of my time than your whole life is worth.' In this he parallels Nelson, whose authority, although total and based on professional brilliance, was enhanced by humanity and consideration for his subordinates, but with no tolerance of incompetence. Like Nelson, Brunel devised the strategy, supervised the tactics and put himself alongside those taking the most severe risks.

ABOVE LEFT The Clifton Suspension Bridge in Bristol embodies many recurrent themes of Brunel's life. Built at a time of intense competition between ports, Brunel submitted his radical design in a competition with Thomas Telford (1757–1834) and others. Due to social unrest and funding problems, however, it was not built until after his death. Other surviving memorials to Brunel include the Royal Albert Bridge at Saltash, the Thames Tunnel at Rotherhithe, and Paddington Station in London.

ABOVE The SS *Great Britain*, the first ever propeller-driven, ocean-going ship, was built in Bristol and launched in 1843. She is now undergoing restoration in the same dry dock in Bristol in which she was built.

The best example of a trusted subordinate was that of the
21-year-old Daniel Gooch (1816–89), appointed by Brunel to be chief
locomotive assistant of the Great Western Railway. Employed initially
by Robert Stephenson, Gooch became convinced that Brunel's prefer-
ence for a broad-gauge railway track of 7′ instead of the standard
gauge of 4′ 8½″ was the solution to fast, efficient and comfortable
trains. Gooch's loyalty to Brunel extended beyond his employer's
death, and it was fitting that he supervised the laying of the first
transatlantic cable in 1865 from Brunel's *Great Eastern*. In his portrait,
Gooch appears far removed from the environment of his working
life, posing as a landed gentleman, complete with glossy dog, only
a delicate pair of dividers giving a clue to his profession. The impres-
sive, puritanical Gooch had this to say of Brunel:

> By his death the greatest of England's engineers was lost, the man
> with the greatest originality of thought and power of execution,
> bold in his plans but right. The commercial world thought him
> extravagant; but although he was so, great things are not done by
> those who sit down and count the cost of every thought and act.

In the same year that he was photographed by Howlett, Brunel
was also painted by his brother-in-law, John Callcott Horsley

Sir Marc Isambard Brunel (1769–1849)
Samuel Drummond, c.1835
Oil on canvas, 1270 × 1016mm (50 × 40″)
National Portrait Gallery, London (NPG 89)

I. K. Brunel's French father, Marc, was a brilliant engineer who built the world's first tunnel through soft ground under a river. Despite Marc Brunel's invention of the tunnelling shield, to protect men whilst working, the building of the Thames Tunnel was beset by problems and deaths, taking from 1825 to 1842 to complete. His son took over as chief engineer on the project, aged only twenty-one.

(1817–1903). Brunel looks up at us from his desk in an unremarkable image, from which the cares of the engineer and the scope of his ambitions are absent. Compared to the Howlett photograph it is anodyne, with no iconic force. Horsley was painting a man he knew well and liked, the family member and private person, rather than the mover of mountains. The survival of this portrait alongside the Howlett image allows us to see a gentler side of Brunel, such as his friends and family might have witnessed in his few moments of repose; but we must remember that, for all his being married, Brunel knew he was not a family man: 'My profession is after all,' he wrote, 'my only fit wife.'

Iron memorials

The memories of the great engineers live on in their surviving structures. Paddington Station and the railway lines to Bristol and the far west of England are still there, frequently the subject of the sort of politico-administrative buck-passing from which Brunel and his contemporaries also suffered. Thirty years ago, his *Great Britain* came home to Bristol from her long exile in the Falkland Islands, her iron hull with its innovative longitudinal strengthening having resisted a century of neglect. Great bridges remain at Clifton and Saltash. Often forgotten is the Thames Tunnel, now carrying the revamped East London branch of the London Underground; the project belonged to his distinguished father, Marc Isambard Brunel (1769–1849), but was the first great theatre of Isambard's technical fertility, personal courage and heroic leadership, as he battled floods and dragged workmates to safety.

Into the *Great Eastern* episode, though, are concentrated the essentials of his reputation: visionary enterprise exploring the limits of contemporary technology; shrinking the globe to the distance that can be travelled with one load of coal; squarely facing and over-coming the problems thrown up by his ambition, only for other problems to present themselves; the project endangered by the inadequacy of men morally and professionally inferior to him; the unswerving loyalty of his chosen subordinates and the comradely generosity he inspired in his professional rivals. It is all there, in the photograph, carrying his reputation over time, a monument as cunningly wrought and enduring as any iron bridge.

Charles Darwin

When Charles Darwin suggested that humans and apes might have evolved from common ancestors, he helped to rewrite history. His theory of evolution by natural selection continues to provoke debate

'Without Darwin's breakthrough idea, we cannot understand life's amazing variety, its history, and our own place in the story of this planet'
Andrew Marr, BBC political editor

We have many local heroes in Britain – special people for these islands to raise our glasses to as the nights draw in. But Charles Darwin is our only world-changer. This kindly, cautious man who lived a hard and sometimes tragic life has given all humanity a bigger, more useful, more relevant thought than any other person in modern times. Variation through natural selection – what we tend just to call evolution these days – is the inner secret of life on earth. Without Darwin's breakthrough idea, we cannot understand life's amazing variety, its history, and our own place in the story of this planet. More, we cannot begin to grapple properly with our human duty to preserve biodiversity and to understand some of the greatest threats ahead. Some 120 years after he died, he bestrides the planet and is still busy remaking our future.

Unlike so many 'great' people, who turn out to be self-certain bullies or simply born in the right place at the right time, Charles Darwin's greatness consists of mental courage – a commitment to truth so strong that he kept thinking his way forward when every instinct told him 'Stop now'. He was born into a world that most Christians accepted had been created by God in 4004 BC, and whose creatures were made, perfect and complete, at the same time. By the time he died, we knew that the world was in constant flux and species were constantly changing and all interrelated.

Darwin came from a line of poets, manufacturers and freethinkers, and as a boy was fascinated by botany, collecting beetles, experimenting with gases and reading avidly. He was meant to be a doctor and was sent to Edinburgh to study medicine at a time when it was the most intellectually exciting city in the world. But he was squeamish and turned instead to the radical new science stirring around him. His father then sent him to Cambridge, hoping to turn this troublesome youth into a parson.

Instead, he carried on with science and within a couple of years, in 1831 got the chance of a lifetime. A small Royal Navy ship, the HMS *Beagle*, was about to sail for South America and possibly all around the world. The captain, Robert FitzRoy, was melancholic and needed a companion. Would Darwin come? He certainly would. As the voyage proceeded, Darwin sent his growing collections of birds, animals and plants back to England. He shuddered at the cruelty and slavery of South America. When he reached the remote Galapagos Islands in the Pacific, the first seeds of his great discovery were planted: the birds and curious animals, including giant tortoises and iguanas, were unlike those anywhere else, and different on each island. Why? Darwin struggled with the idea for years before he was finally sure.

By then, he was living in Kent and married, a successful scientist and well-known author. Like many Victorians, he suffered terribly from the deaths of children: when his favourite daughter Annie died in agony at ten, and despite having been trained for the Anglican priesthood, his Christian faith was finally shattered. He suffered too from painful and debilitating illness. Yet he never stopped working, studying everything from earthworms to orchids, coral reefs to the facial expressions of children and monkeys, as he struggled to master the secrets of how life kept changing, and why.

At the moment when Darwin was finally convinced that he understood the truth, he wrote to a friend telling him, 'it is like confessing a murder'. For years he had kept the great secret hidden, struggling to perfect it and to deal with all possible objections. It was only when another scientist came up with a very similar theory, partly thanks to Darwin's encouragement, that he was driven into publication. Once published, however, *The Origin of Species* – still a vivid, very readable book – became an instant bestseller, and Darwin

Charles Darwin 1809–82

12 February 1809	Born at The Mount in Shrewsbury, England
1825–7	Studies at Edinburgh University to become a physician, in the tradition of father and grandfather – more interested in natural history than medicine
1831–6	Invited by Captain Robert FitzRoy to be unpaid naturalist aboard the HMS *Beagle*, about to begin a five-year circumnavigation of the globe
1836–44	Darwin produces a series of notebooks on biology, recording ideas and facts relative to the origin and transformation of species
1839	Darwin marries Emma Wedgwood, with whom he has ten children. Darwin's first book, *Journal of Research*, is published
1839–43	*Zoology of the Voyage of HMS Beagle*, edited by Darwin, is published in five volumes
1854–8	Writes an encyclopaedic work on barnacles (following eight years' study of the creature), followed by his 'Big Book' on species transmutation, over 2,000 pages in length
18 June 1858	Darwin receives letter from Alfred Russell Wallace, who has formulated a theory of evolution through natural selection: Wallace's key concepts seem to reflect the very chapter titles of the draft version of Darwin's as yet unpublished *Origin*
1 July 1858	Papers by Darwin and Wallace, announcing theory of evolution through natural selection, are read at Linnaean Society, London
1859	*The Origin of Species* is published and sells 1,250 copies on the first day
1859–82	Darwin continues his quiet life of research and writing in Downe. Publishes five further editions of *The Origin of Species* plus other works related to the topic and seven volumes on plants and worms
19 April 1882	Charles Darwin dies, aged 73, at Down House, Downe, Kent

went on to grapple directly with mankind's place in nature. He knew full well that a small, slimy mollusc had evolved, over rather a long time, into Anglican clergymen, whales and parrots . . . but this knowledge was not popular with the Victorian establishment. When the prime minister of the day suggested him for a knighthood, Queen Victoria (1819–1901), on the advice of her bishops, refused. Darwinism was held to be undignified. It dethroned God and made monkeys of men. Darwin disagreed. For him, the truth came first, and was beautiful. There was, he said, 'grandeur in this view of life . . . that whilst this planet has gone on cycling according to the fixed law of gravity, from so simple a beginning endless forms most beautiful and most wonderful have been, and are being, evolved.'

Since then, his great idea has been shaken, hacked at, abused and mocked. Great thinkers and respected scientists have done their utmost to destroy it. Fundamentalists have scorned it. Even today, in the United States more people believe that the world was created in seven days by God than accept Darwinism; and Britain too has schools teaching 'Creationism' rather than the truth. Yet real science shows again and again that far from natural selection weakening, it is in fact even stronger and faster than Darwin himself

realised. His thinking soaks into psychology (as he predicted it would) and, via genetics, into great arguments about the very future of humanity. He was not an environmentalist – nor then was anyone else – but his understanding of the complicated, delicate interconnection of all living things is essential to modern, 'green' thought. All sorts of politicians, from Marxists to Nazis, have tried to claim Darwinism as their own, but the old man has seen them all off. As it happens, he was a humane, open-minded moderate in politics, who abhorred slavery and extremism.

Darwin was great because he had the courage not to stop thinking, not to flinch, when his thought was tearing down the mental world he lived in. But to honour Darwin is to honour this country too. Our best inheritance – the freedom to think, write and speak, to travel, to argue publicly, to enjoy free society and the free market – was what made Darwin and Darwinism. What he did could have been done in very few other countries 150 years ago – and not all countries even now. What he gave, this great discovery, he gave to the world. But finding it in the first place – that was also about Britain in the nineteenth century, at her young, impatient, energetic best.

The image of a naturalist

'Man with all his noble qualities ... still bears in his bodily frame
the indelible stamp of his lowly origin.'

CHARLES DARWIN, *The Descent of Man* (1871), closing words

Charles Darwin
Elliot and Fry, 1874
Colourised photograph, 83 × 55mm (3¼ × 2⅛")
The Natural History Museum, London

Early photographs chart the receding, greying hair
exposing the broad forehead above craggy brows,
deep-set eyes, strong nose and wide mouth.
Following the publication of *The Origin of Species*
in 1859, with its attendant controversy and his
growing fame, Darwin retreated behind a full beard.
This gave temporary anonymity until photographs
of his hirsute venerability assured his iconic status.

In the early decades of the nineteenth century, evolutionary theories
were proliferating. Ordinary people – far too many of them for the
establishment's liking – were showing an interest in these challenging
ideas, and then, to make matters worse, along came Robert Chambers
(1802–71), a magazine journalist and popular writer on scientific
topics. His *Vestiges of the Natural History of Creation*, published in 1844,
was a bestseller, absorbed enthusiastically for its intoxicating
suggestion that Nature developed through its own devices, through
a transmutatory process divorced from any direct divine intervention.
This was levelling stuff, reducing the authority of God, and therefore
with serious implications for the privileges of his official representatives on (British) earth, the ordained clergy of the Church of England.
Many of these Anglicans were part- or full-time natural philosophers
or 'scientists' – botanists, geologists, entomologists – and had influential friends with similar interests among the upper-middle-class
gentlemen who shared with them the management of public and
academic science at Oxford and Cambridge universities and through
them the various learned societies.

Challenging the Church of England

The view of the establishment was that Chambers had to be sorted
out. His book went through several editions, despite the savage
review of the Reverend Adam Sedgwick (1785–1873), a blunt Yorkshire
geologist, who lambasted the coupling, in an 'unlawful marriage',
of evolution and spontaneous generation and the consequent
spawning of a hideous monster; he advised people to crush 'the
head of the filthy abortion, and put an end to its crawlings'. So the
religio-scientific establishment invited Robert Chambers to the 1847
meeting of the British Association for the Advancement of Science,
held that year in Oxford, where, in a very churchy lecture hall, the
assembled lions duly savaged the brave journalist. A witness to this

ABOVE **Emma Darwin** (1808–96) aged about fifty after bearing her tenth child
Unknown artist, published by Elliot and Fry, 1860
Photograph, 58 × 92mm (2¼ × 3⅝")
Darwin Archive, Cambridge University Library

A devout Christian and loving wife, Emma Darwin often nursed her dyspeptic husband. She regretted that his work was 'putting God further off', and that his loss of faith barred them from eternal life together.

ABOVE RIGHT **British Association for the Advancement of Science meeting at Oxford University, 1847**, published in 1847
Illustrated London News

Herbert Ingram founded the *Illustrated London News*, the world's first illustrated news magazine, in 1842. It reported and illustrated a wide range of national and international affairs, and the inclusion of scientific events – the more controversial the better – aroused and confirmed public interest. Circulation rose from an initial 26,000 to 300,000 in 1863.

event was Charles Darwin, a friend and former pupil of Sedgwick's at Cambridge, securely embedded in the social world of gentlemanly natural philosophy, but carrying in his pocket a piece of heresy more profoundly scientific and dangerous than Chambers's squib: his first tentative essay outlining what became his theory of natural selection.

Darwin was at the lecture hall partly to meet his friend and intellectual sounding-board, the botanist Joseph Dalton Hooker (1817–1911), and to gauge the younger man's reaction to his developing theory. Darwin respected Hooker's science, trusted his intellectual honesty and felt closer to him than other practitioners because Hooker too had made an extensive voyage of collection and discovery. Darwin had confessed to Hooker in January 1844 that he was engaged in 'a very presumptuous work', based on observation and analysis of thousands of specimens and readings in 'heaps of agricultural & horticultural books'; he had become 'almost convinced (quite contrary to the opinion I started with) that species are not . . . immutable.'

Thus, hesitatingly, self-deprecatingly, he broached his great concern in a letter to his new friend. Hooker did not disappoint, and became a 'co-opted assistant in Darwin's quest for the laws of life'.

Powerful allies

It does not diminish Darwin's achievement to remind ourselves of his reliance on collaborators. His judgement in trusting Hooker so early in their relationship was intuitively brilliant; the forty years of their intellectual and personal relationship, a meeting of tough minds and not without its fierce disagreements, is a tribute to the rigour and magnanimity of both men. A key element of the relationship was the dynamic arising from the social difference between the two men. Darwin was a wealthy, independent gentleman; he had taken up scientific pursuits initially as a leisure interest, to fill the spare hours of the country parson he nearly became. Hooker's father was the distinguished Sir William Hooker (1785–1865), Director of the Royal Botanic Gardens at Kew, a salaried professional. When Joseph went on his voyage of scientific discovery, he did so as a salaried Royal Navy assistant surgeon; Darwin had gone as gentleman companion to

ABOVE LEFT **Charles Darwin**
Maull and Polyblank, c.1855
Albumen print, 200 × 146mm (7⅞ × 5¾")
National Portrait Gallery, London (NPG P106 (7))

ABOVE **Joseph Dalton Hooker** (1817–1911)
Maull and Polyblank, c.1855
Albumen print, 200 × 146mm (7⅞ × 5¾")
National Portrait Gallery, London (NPG P106 (12))

Darwin was inhibited about promoting his ideas: he feared controversy would damage his social status, and he was a poor debater. He provided the intellectual ammunition and background support to expert scientific polemicists such as Joseph Hooker and, above all, Thomas Huxley who took the fight for natural selection into the lecture halls and learned societies, and into print. Huxley's ire was often directed at the powerful anti-Darwinian Richard Owen, hating his 'metaphorical mystifications' masquerading as science. Whenever possible Owen pulled rank over the younger Huxley, once assuming the title 'Professor' to give a series of lectures in Huxley's own School of Mines, thereby undermining his authority.

Captain FitzRoy of HMS *Beagle*, paying his own way. Darwin remained a private man, driven by the imperatives of his class to maintain a position of respectable independence. Hooker became as distinguished a professional as his father and worked as his deputy at Kew before succeeding him as Director. Darwin's theories were anathema to the traditional, Oxbridge-based scientific establishment of the late 1830s and 1840s and also to many of his social equals; but as keen, secular, London-based professionals like Hooker, aided by sympathetic journals such as the *Westminster Review*, gradually shifted the intellectual balance in favour of evolutionary thought during the 1850s, and as they became more senior in bodies like the Royal Society and the Royal Institution, the ground was prepared for the introduction of Darwin's big idea.

One of the promoters of London-based professional science at that time was Thomas Huxley (1825–95), an ambitious, energetic young biologist, 27-years-old in 1852 and already a Fellow of the Royal Society, but hard-up and unable to persuade anyone to give him a job. A fine scientist in his own right, he was an even better polemicist, a muscular street fighter for the secularisation of science, strongly influenced by the theories of Herbert Spencer (1820–1903) on social evolution towards the perfecting of mankind. Huxley met Darwin in April 1853, and over the next six years was regularly in touch, in between fierce wars against establishment figures such as the prestigious zoologist Sir Richard Owen (1804–92). Darwin always worried about Huxley's vehemence, commenting after one bout with Owen, 'Your father confessor trembles for you.' Darwin was aware of how effective an ally the pugnacious young man could be, and cultivated him assiduously as one whose aggressive tactics might play a role in his strategy for presenting the theory of natural selection.

Darwinian disciples

When *The Origin of Species* was published in 1859, Darwin's supporters were ready in sufficient force, notably in scientific institutions and with access to the serious press (Huxley reviewed it for *The Times*), to join battle with the forces of conservatism. It is clear that Darwin, in his careful dealings with his publisher John Murray, by his lobbying of distinguished – and in this case continually wavering – old friends like Sir Charles Lyell (1797–1875), and above all by motivating his disciples, had done much to prepare the ground. It would be a mistake

Thomas Henry Huxley (1825–95)
John Collier, c.1883
Oil on canvas, 1270 × 1016mm (50 × 40")
National Portrait Gallery, London (NPG 3168)

Sir Richard Owen (1804–92)
Maull and Polyblank, c.1855
Albumen print, arched top,
200 × 146mm (7⅞ × 5¾")
National Portrait Gallery, London (NPG P106 (15))

Samuel Wilberforce (1805–73)
Carlo Pellegrini, published in *Vanity Fair*, 24 July, 1869
Watercolour, 305 × 181mm (12 × 7⅛")
National Portrait Gallery, London (NPG 1993)

The son of William, the anti-slavery reformer, Samuel was Bishop of Oxford at the height of *The Origin of Species* controversy. At the 1860 meeting of the British Association for the Advancement of Science, held in Oxford, he debated with Darwin's supporters Hooker and Huxley. Defending the establishment position that science was a branch of theology presided over by an all-creating God, 'Soapy Sam' angered Huxley, who railed against 'the round-mouthed, oily, special pleading of the man'.

to carry too far the image of Darwin as an unworldly naturalist, bemused by the storm that broke over his head.

He was, however, no public speaker, for as he said himself, 'it is something unintelligible to me how anyone can argue in public like orators do . . . I am glad I was not in Oxford, for I should have been overwhelmed.' The Oxford meeting that Darwin refers to was the 1860 meeting of the British Association for the Advancement of Science. This was the great set-piece confrontation between the Darwinists and the old guard, widely reported, and a key event in publicising and polarising the arguments for and against Darwin's theories. The keynote speaker for the traditionalists was the Bishop of Oxford, Samuel Wilberforce (1805–73), who famously baited Huxley by asking him if it was on his grandfather's or his grandmother's side that he was descended from an ape. Huxley, according to eye-witnesses, was white with anger, and Hooker reported that his response was inaudible. Huxley's own version presents him as calm under fire, retorting that he would rather have an ape for a grandfather than a rich and clever man who abused his privileges 'for the purpose of introducing ridicule into a grave scientific discussion'.

The fight was on, and over four hundred books and pamphlets were published during the next five years. Huxley was prominent in this activity: his series of lectures, delivered at the School of Mines in London and to audiences of working people in Edinburgh, and published as *Man's Place in Nature*, made explicit the implications for human ancestry raised in *The Origin of Species* and won a whole new constituency for Darwin, preparing the ground for his *The Descent of Man* (1871). The monkey–man link popularised the argument: 'Is Man an Ape or an Angel?' asked a rhetorical Benjamin Disraeli (1804–81), before answering, 'My Lord, I am on the side of the Angels.' Darwin himself enjoyed the prevailing mood, expressing disappointment that his old friend and mentor Sir Charles Lyell, unable to accept the absence of some degree of divine intervention in the evolutionary process, 'would not go the whole orang'.

Fundamental debate

There was a deftness about Darwin's positioning of himself throughout the whole controversy that did much to protect his reputation, both in his own time and subsequently. He had to balance two things: the preservation of his and his family's respectability, and

RIGHT **'A Sun of the Nineteenth Century'**
Unknown artist, published in Pack, NY, 1882
Darwin Archive, Cambridge University Library

This illustration depicts Darwin as the 'secular sun'
of the scientific enlightenment, driving out the
spiritual darkness of religion and attendant
ignorance, represented by the Pope, priests and
the English Bible.

BELOW **Charles Darwin as a Monkey**
Faustin Betheder 'Faustin', undated
Coloured lithograph, 141 × 66mm (5½ × 2½")
National Portrait Gallery, London (NPG D1388)

THE
LONDON SKETCH BOOK.

PROF. DARWIN.

This is the ape of form.
Love's Labor Lost. act 5, scene 2.

Some four or five descents since.
All's Well that Ends Well. act 3, sc. 7.

an appropriate dissemination of his potentially blasphemous ideas. He was quite happy that Huxley should lecture to working men and consort with atheistic political radicals, but the 'Sage of Down' was wary. The best example of this is in his avoidance of the atheist MP Charles Bradlaugh (1833–91) and his collaborator, the freethinking feminist Annie Besant (1847–1933). In 1876 they sought Darwin's public approval for 'Fruits of Philosophy', a pamphlet on birth control; Darwin demurred, fearing that the family unit that he so much treasured for both social and personal reasons would be endangered and that would be the 'greatest of all possible threats to mankind'. Four years later he brushed Bradlaugh and Besant off again, refusing to accept the dedication to him of a series of evolutionary articles for the *National Reformer.* An impressionable visitor to Darwin's home found him 'picturesque', and with that we might agree – but not with the same observer's view that he had 'guileless simplicity'.

The fight has been going on ever since. The main opposition in the last hundred years has come from the forces of Christian fundamentalism in the United States of America. In 1925, the famous 'Monkey Trial' captured headlines far beyond Dayton, Tennessee. A science teacher, John Scopes, had attempted to teach evolution, which was then against the law in a number of Southern states; the liberal lawyer Clarence Darrow (1857–1938) represented him, against a fundamentalist ex-presidential candidate, William Jennings Bryan (1860–1925). The evolutionists lost on a technicality, but the international exposure did much to promote the cause of Darwinism, and to stir up its defenders in the United States. Nowadays, academic and religious institutions nail their virtual colours to the mast and wage a worldwide war. The Institute for Creation Research will sell you a video to 'learn why evolution contradicts the most widely accepted laws of science making evolution scientifically impossible'. Also based in California, The National Center for Science Education, alarmed that only 44 per cent of adult Americans agree that humans developed from the earliest species of animals, provides arguments and resources in support of Darwinian evolution in the public schools.

Victorian heroes

A photograph of Darwin presides over many of the websites, a patriarchal figure whose likeness to an Old Testament prophet might be thought to reassure literal interpreters of the Bible. The photograph most used was taken by Julia Margaret Cameron (1815–79); the Darwins rented a holiday house from her in 1869, and she took the opportunity to add Darwin to a list of intellectual heavyweights that included Thomas Carlyle (1795–1881) and Lord Tennyson (1809–92), a deliberate celebration of high achievers. Darwin stated his approval of her work, and from this and the many other photographs of him we can conclude that, if not an active publicity seeker, he certainly contributed to the dissemination of his own image. He sat for several *carte-de-visite* photographs, a key indicator of Victorian celebrity; for Elliot and Fry he wore his hat and cloak, habitually worn on his constitutionals around the 'sand-walk' at Down House, and also worn in the painting by John Collier (1850–1934), evoking his measured daily routine.

The image of the venerable, bearded sage has proved entirely appropriate: it bears the weight of his ideas in its worn simplicity, and has a resonance denied the slight image of Jane Austen (1777–1817) or the undistinguished Shakespeare portraits. We are fortunate, too, in the survival of earlier images to remind us of his fresh-faced youth, and of what powerful features were masked by the beard. The 1855 photograph by Maull and Polyblank, taken after Darwin completed his great work on barnacles, shows resolution and intensity on his strong, foursquare face.

It was inevitable that he would be both ridiculed and venerated in imagery. The ridicule was easy: cartoonists discovered a simian element in deep-set eyes under a craggy brow, and the increasingly popular illustrated magazines like *Punch* could not resist. If ink was the medium of ridicule, marble was the material of veneration and

Charles Darwin
Elliot and Fry, 1879
Albumen cabinet photo, 305 × 181mm (12 × 7⅛")
National Portrait Gallery, London

These two images reinforce Darwin's heavyweight reputation. The marble by the former Pre-Raphaelite Thomas Woolner dates from as early as c.1869, the permanence of the medium a true reflection of Darwin's contribution to botanical science, through his tenacious methodology as well as his overarching theories. John Collier, who married Thomas Huxley's daughter Marian, painted his first version of this portrait in 1881. By common consent considered 'the best likeness', when the National Portrait Gallery required an image of the scientist in 1883, Collier agreed to copy it. Darwin is shown with the cloak and hat that he wore for his daily constitutionals around the 'sandwalk' at Down House, accessories forming part of his quiet, country-dwelling image. The solemnity of both images reminds us of Richard Dawkins's remark that such is the gravity of Darwin's reputation that, whereas in the US they have 'In God we trust' on their paper money, in Britain we have Darwin.

the indicator of enduring fame, and while we expect and indeed find a proliferation of posthumous statuary, it is significant that Thomas Woolner (1826–92) should have sculpted him for the Botany Department at Cambridge University as early as 1869. Perhaps the latest posthumous statue is that by Jemma Pearson, recently commissioned by Darwin's old school, Shrewsbury, and showing him at the time of his *Beagle* voyage, kitted out for specimen gathering.

It seems fitting to conclude by mentioning three British organisations that perpetuate the memory of Darwin. The library of Cambridge University is engaged upon the Darwin Correspondence Project; by publishing a definitive edition in thirty volumes, this project will deepen our understanding of his intellectual development, working methods and social context. The Natural History Museum in London will open the first phase of its Darwin Centre in

September 2002, in this case using the prestige of Darwin's name for a major contribution to the public understanding of science in general; lastly, English Heritage manages Down House, maintaining the delicate balance between access and conservation.

A secular saint

One more location: Westminster Abbey. The new scientific establishment was determined that their secular saint, the provider of their most potent doctrine, should rest in the pantheon of British greatness as a mark of his achievement, but also as a demonstration of their political and social clout. It was a sign that they were now an integral part of the wider British establishment, which had, appropriately, evolved sufficiently to absorb, or at least to accommodate, within its official church what had once been dangerously radical and blasphemous ideas. Darwin had made this process easier by his reticence on religious issues, another example of his political deftness and of his personal sensitivity in respecting his wife Emma's sincere Christianity. There is a degree of reciprocation here: Darwin had relied on the minds and energy of his fellow scientists to promote his ideas, and they used his body to demonstrate that science was no longer a genteel extension of theology, but a dynamic, independent, intellectual tool for the shaping of the world. Where that left God, many were uncertain, but it did no harm to Darwin.

ABOVE LEFT **Charles Darwin's Study at Down House** English Heritage

ABOVE **The Darwin Centre, Phase One, at the Natural History Museum, London, 2002**

Darwin's achievements are commemorated in institutions named after him. Some, like the Natural History Museum's new Darwin Centre, celebrate his influence in the field of natural science; others, like the interdisciplinary Darwin College, Cambridge, more generally. Perhaps his best memorial is the development of his ideas in the minds of contemporary scientists.

OPPOSITE
Charles Darwin
Julia Margaret Cameron, 1868
Albumen print, 330 × 256mm (13 × 10⅛")
National Portrait Gallery, London (NPG P8)

Julia Margaret Cameron took to photography in middle age, having been given some equipment by her family. Through experimenting, she realised the aesthetic potential of variable focus and dramatic lighting. A formidable personality, she persuaded many leading, mid-Victorian male intellectuals to pose for her, celebrating their hirsute gravity in the same spirit that the founders of the National Portrait Gallery chose to record them. Thomas Carlyle, Alfred Lord Tennyson, G. F. Watts and Sir John Herschel were amongst her sitters.

Winston Churchill

As Prime Minister of Britain during the
Second World War, Winston Churchill was
a defiant leader who encouraged the people,
the government, and the armed forces to
believe that victory was possible

'Churchill was instinctive, daring, often infuriating . . . but he was also an inspiration. Thanks to him, Britain lived on'

Mo Mowlam, politician

In the summer of 1940, Britain stood alone on the brink of invasion. At that crucial time, one man, Winston Churchill, defined what it meant to be British. We like to think of ourselves as tolerant and long-suffering people. But Churchill, through his leadership and his example, reminded us that if all we hold dear – our democracy, our freedom – is threatened, we will show courage and determination like no other nation:

> I have nothing to offer but blood, toil, tears and sweat. You ask what is our policy? I can say: it is to wage war by sea, land and air, with all our might and with all our strength that God can give us; to wage war against a monstrous tyranny, never surpassed in the dark, lamentable catalogue of human crime. You ask what is our aim? I can answer in one word: it is victory, victory at all costs, victory in spite of all terror, victory however long and hard the road may be.

This was the moment when Britain had to be at its greatest. And in Churchill we found the greatest of Britons.

Winston Churchill was born in 1874 into one of Britain's grandest families. The Churchills had been fighting for king and country for generations. Young Winston always believed he'd do the same. But self-belief was something he maintained despite rather than because of his family. His father, Lord Randolph Churchill (1849–95), and his mother, Jennie (1854–1921), were both cold and distant people. Winston was packed off to Harrow. He wasn't good-looking or clever; he was sickly, with a lisp and a stammer. He was bound to be bullied – and he was. Far from giving him support, Winston's father predicted his child would 'degenerate into a shabby, unhappy and futile existence'.

He left school and, after three attempts, got into the military academy at Sandhurst. After Sandhurst he went looking for military action – wherever it was. He paid for himself by doubling up as a war correspondent. He used his dispatches to promote himself as a hero of the Boer War, and returned to England in 1900 renowned and all set to become an MP.

He was elected as Tory MP for Oldham in the same year. Then he swapped to the Liberals, then back. He was never really a Party animal. He cared about Britain. His vision was of a place with better living standards for ordinary people, but a fierce regard for law and order. Though he wasn't a vicious man, Churchill's attitude towards suffragettes, trade unionists or anyone who challenged the system was brutal. His weapon of first resort was the army.

But then he'd always wanted to be a general. This ambition dated back to the days when he spent his school holidays playing with toy soldiers in the corridors of Blenheim Palace, below the tapestries of his heroic ancestors. He must have been delighted when, in 1911, he was made First Lord of the Admiralty – and even more so when the First World War offered him the opportunity to plan a major military offensive at Gallipoli, in 1915.

Gallipoli was a disaster, costing Winston his job and nearly his sanity. This was the onset of his first major bout of depression, a curse he called his 'black dog'. Thankfully he now had a wife, Clementine, to help him through it. She was eleven years younger than him, beautiful, clever and unswervingly loyal. She kept him together, but he got himself out of it, in true Churchillian fashion. To make amends for his mistake, he took himself off to the trenches of France to fight. He must be one of the few soldiers to have written home from the First World War that he had 'found happiness and content such as I have not known for months'. He was a man made for war.

By the time Churchill returned to England, he'd already

Winston Churchill 1874–1965

30 November 1874	Born at Blenheim Palace, Oxfordshire, to Lord Randolph (1849–95) and Lady Churchill (Jennie Jerome) (1854–1921)
1 September 1893	Enters Royal Military College, Sandhurst, as a cavalry cadet
20 February 1895	Commissioned into the 4th Queen's Own Hussars
1 October 1900	Elected to the House of Commons as Conservative MP for Oldham, aged twenty-five
1906	Elected as a Liberal MP for North-West Manchester
1910	Appointed Home Secretary but loses seat in Parliament in 1922. Re-elected in 1924
1932–8	Churchill warns Britain about Hitler and Germany
1939	Britain declares war on Germany: Second World War begins
10 May 1940	Appointed Prime Minister
8 May 1945	Churchill announces the end of Second World War in Europe. In July 1945 Churchill resigns as Prime Minister but returns to this post in October 1951
1953	Knighted by Queen Elizabeth II in July and receives the Nobel Prize for Literature in October
1955	Resigns as Prime Minister
24 January 1965	Dies at his home, 28 Hyde Park Gate, London, at the age of ninety

achieved many great things. He'd been a successful journalist, he'd fought for his country and he'd held high office, as he was to do again in the 1920s as Chancellor of the Exchequer. But by 1930, Labour was in power and he was on the backbenches, a nobody and a has-been. He largely sat out the 1930s at his country retreat, Chartwell.

In September 1938, Prime Minister Neville Chamberlain (1869–1940) famously brandished an agreement he'd signed with Adolf Hitler (1889–1945) and declared he'd secured peace in our time. You could almost hear the sighs of relief. But not from Winston. He'd predicted – long before anyone else – what German nationalism was leading to. By the time he was proved right, and war had been declared, King George VI (1895–1952) knew that 'there was only one person I could send for to form a Government who had the confidence of the country. And that was Winston.' When the call came, Churchill was 65-years-old. It had been a long wait, but destiny had arrived.

People talk of 1066, of the Armada, of Trafalgar. But 1940 was the most important year in British history. It was the year of Dunkirk, the Battle of Britain, the Blitz. It was the year when every single Briton, civilian as well as soldier, found themselves at war. The cause appeared hopeless, yet Winston, reviving the V sign of victory from the fields of Agincourt five hundred years before, told us we could win.

Churchill was an instinctive, daring, often infuriating war leader. He was rude and unpleasant to his staff, who struggled to keep up with his limitless capacity for hard work and hard liquor. But he was also an inspiration. When victory was finally declared in Europe on 8 May 1945, it was quickly followed by a general election. The billboards said 'Cheer Churchill, Vote Labour', and that's what people did. That was the irony. The very democracy that Churchill was prepared to lay down his life to defend was the same democracy that knew the difference between the needs of peace and the needs of war.

When Churchill died in 1965, the new rock-and-roll Britain stood still. If Britain – its eccentricity, its strength of character, its big-heartedness – had to be summed up in one person, it was him. He had gone, but, thanks to him, Britain lived on. And what could be greater than that?

The image of a leader

'To succeed pre-eminently in English public life it is necessary to conform either to the popular image of a bookie or of a clergyman; Churchill being a perfect example of the former, Halifax of the latter.'

MALCOLM MUGGERIDGE (1903–90), *The Infernal Grove* (1973)

Winston Churchill
Robert Elliot, 1945
Bromide print, 252 × 202mm (9⅞ × 8")
National Portrait Gallery, London (NPG x17071)

Churchill's simple gesture inspired hope, signalled defiance, and celebrated eventual victory. Its similarity to a well-used digital insult rendered it doubly effective as a morale booster. After fifty years in politics, Churchill was a skilful popular communicator: gestures, expressions, hats, various uniforms and other sartorial eccentricities supplemented verbal mastery.

Most leading politicians position themselves for posterity through published memoirs: there they justify contentious decisions, settle scores, acknowledge or defend failures, and selectively present their personal 'hinterland' of influences and associations in whatever way they think will reflect on them best. Winston Churchill eschewed such a restricted format: he did not limit himself to the narrow canvas of a self-portrait, but chose instead to depict an awesome panorama of conflict and co-operation covering the two world wars, in which he was a central and often controlling character. As Churchill himself said to his research assistant Sir William Deakin: 'This is not history, this is my case.' And the historian Sir John Plumb reminded us in *Churchill: Four Faces and the Man* (1969) that historians since 1945, seeking a path through the mass of material, 'have moved down the broad avenues which he drove through war's confusion and complexity'.

Foreign correspondent

This process of writing about conflict – and including himself in it – began with Churchill's very earliest work as a war correspondent in the 1890s, when, although a serving Army officer, he supplemented his pay and experiences by reporting back to various papers on Britain's imperial wars. Bumptious, pushy and an adept string-puller through his political and social connections, he elbowed his way to the scene of the fighting and sent back exciting, literate despatches in which his own experiences featured significantly; in addition, he produced more considered material – magazine articles, lectures and books – in which he discussed issues of imperial policy and, as in *The River War* (1899), made trenchant criticisms of the conduct of campaigns. Much of this was for the money, but it was also to establish, on his terms and above all in his language, a reputation as a participant, interpreter and, by implication, a potential director of the great imperial adventure.

ABOVE **Winston Churchill**
Lyddell Sawyer, 1901
Albumen print, 143 × 103mm (5⅝ × 4")
National Portrait Gallery, London (NPG P705)

ABOVE RIGHT **Winston Churchill**
Walter Richard Sickert, 1927
Oil on canvas, 457 × 305mm (18 × 12")
National Portrait Gallery, London (NPG 4438)

Churchill was a good amateur artist and enjoyed learning from professionals. Both Walter Sickert and Graham Sutherland, when painting him at Chartwell, were pumped for advice. The portraits by Sir William Orpen, particularly, and Sir John Lavery, painted during the First World War, won his approval. But it was photographs that defined his popular image, from the truculent prisoner of the Boers to spreads in *Picture Post*, in planes, boats, trains, beds and wheelchairs, from bumptious officer of hussars to Beaton's and Karsh's icon of defiance.

These early experiences and the income they provided launched his political career. If he had died in 1939, at the age of sixty-five, that career might well have been judged a failure: high office had been achieved, but his tenures had been punctuated by failures and misjudgements, such as the disastrous Dardanelles military expedition of 1915 and the return to the gold standard in the late 1920s. In opposition during the 1930s he had become isolated from his Conservative colleagues over their support for a move towards dominion status for India. His isolation was increased both by his opposition to the rising threat of Nazi Germany when, as the historian Andrew Roberts has demonstrated in *Eminent Churchillians* (1994), the monarchy and the Conservative political and social elite supported the appeasement of the Nazi regime, and by his reputation as a political adventurer with a cavalier attitude to party loyalty. Roberts also reminds us that it took a full fourteen months after Churchill's appointment as Prime Minister in 1940, during the darkest hours of the war, for the 'undeclared guerrilla war' between him and the Conservative elite to die down. Much of this, of course, was forgotten after the war, once Churchill had become

Alan Brooke, 1st Viscount Alanbrooke (1883–1963)
Yousuf Karsh, 1943
Bromide print, 494 × 394mm (19⅜ × 15½")
National Portrait Gallery, London (NPG P490(1))

Most of Churchill's close colleagues during the war years recorded their impressions in some form. Alanbrooke, the military chief, admired and loved him, but vented frustrations in his diaries. Attlee, appreciative of his overall leadership, was similarly exasperated by Churchill's unsystematic approach to committee work and reliance on favoured individuals. More junior figures also left records: Sir John Colville, Churchill's private secretary, wrote a detailed and informative diary, highly rated by historians, as did Sir Henry 'Chips' Channon. Future Prime Ministers Anthony Eden and Harold Macmillan reminisced in memoirs about their political godfather.

an acknowledged national hero and the Conservatives burnished his reputation along with their own.

Breadth of vision

At the beginning of this twenty-first century, sixty years after the Second World War, we still look back in amazement at what Churchill achieved between 1940 and 1945. All manner of revisionism has been undertaken; young historians have dared to stray from the broad Churchillian avenues, investigating byways and secret places that the great man avoided; the vast resources available on his life and times have been ransacked and analysed: and yet he is not significantly diminished. We must agree with David Reynolds, writing in *Churchill* (R. Blake and W. R. Louis, eds. 1996), that 'the Churchill of 1940, his finest hour, is great enough to survive both the hagiographers and the historians'. If anything, admiration of the quality of his personal leadership – the courage, vitality, magnanimity and breadth of vision that simplified the complex issues of a world war – has increased as more detailed evidence has been made available and interpreted.

A good example of this can be found in the recently published complete war diaries of Field-Marshal Lord Alanbrooke (1883–1963), Chief of the Imperial General Staff 1941–6. Lord Alanbrooke (plain Alan Brooke before he was created Baron in 1945 and then Viscount in 1946), a military and political operator of high moral courage, analytical mind and steely integrity, had to contend on an almost daily basis with Churchill's direct interference with military operations, with his romantic view of warfare in which charismatic officers led headline-grabbing assaults on the soft underbelly of the enemy, and with his irregular working habits, drinking, bad temper and pettiness; and yet Brooke loved him for the burden he carried, for his ability to embody and project the resistance of the nation and the certainty of victory, for his grasp of the whole picture, for his humour and indomitable courage. Brooke, one of the finest soldiers this country has produced, was proud to have been Churchill's subordinate. And the US general and Supreme Commander of the Allied forces for the Normandy landings in 1944, Dwight D. Eisenhower (1890–1969), concluded that Churchill 'came nearest to fulfilling the requirements of greatness in any individual that I have met in my lifetime. I have known finer and greater characters, wiser philosophers, more understanding personalities, but no greater man.'

Winston Churchill
Poster – 'Let Us Go Forward Together'
Imperial War Museum, London

Posters were widely used during the Second World War to raise morale. Here a 'V for Victory' formation of fighter aircraft emphasises the defiance of Churchill's spirit and the encouragement of his words.

Clement Attlee, 1st Earl Attlee (1883–1967)
George Harcourt, 1946
Oil on canvas, 794 × 629mm (31¼ × 24¾")
National Portrait Gallery, London (NPG 4593)

V for victory

Brooke and Eisenhower worked alongside Churchill and felt his impact across the conference table. The people of Britain saw him on his visits to damaged cities, to factories and military bases, moved by the suffering that he saw and exuding bulldog resolve; they saw him in the flesh, they saw him on cinema newsreels, they saw him in press and magazine photographs and cartoons, and they heard his eloquent defiance over the radio. It was a remarkable projection: the elderly, Edwardian politician, wearing a series of unusual hats and costumes, cigar in mouth, stick in hand, free hand giving the V for Victory sign to his people, and V for something else to Hitler. This image had some incongruous elements, too: Churchill was an aristocrat, a direct descendant of the first Duke of Marlborough; he was attended by personal servants, had probably never been on a bus and, according to a member of his staff, did not carry any money. He lived remote from the people, yet came to be seen by them as the very embodiment of their insular defiance – a man for the people, not of them.

Tone of voice

Some political sophisticates found Churchill's broadcasts hackneyed. Although it is difficult today to measure response to them, the recordings have been analysed in great detail by historians. He made forty-nine speeches as Prime Minister, lasting from eighty-four seconds to forty-eight minutes, with eleven of the forty-nine lasting less than five minutes. In 1940 he broadcast five speeches between May and September; they were composed laboriously, with some recasting of phrases previously used; the historian David Cannadine has pointed out that the phrase 'so much owed by so many to so few' first appeared in 1899. Maybe – but as the American journalist and broadcaster Edward R. Murrow (1908–65) commented, 'he mobilised the English language and sent it into battle'. In so doing, Churchill's Elizabethan echoes struck a chord; his inspirational patriotism, expressed in somewhat archaic terms, resonated with the people of Britain. 'Let us therefore brace ourselves to our duties, and so bear ourselves that, if the British Empire and its Commonwealth last for a thousand years, men will still say: "This was their finest hour."' Not the language of the pictures, the wireless, the music hall or the pub, but a potent invocation of literary and historical folk-memories, for a

society under attack, where such resonances were undiluted by any sense of national decline or general disillusionment with political leadership. His language worked.

Writing after the war, Churchill remembered the night of 10 May 1940, when King George VI asked him to form a government: 'I felt as if I were walking with destiny, and that all my past life had been but a preparation for this hour and for this trial.' His sense of himself as destined to play a major role in our national history had sustained him through the preceding difficult years. The moment had finally arrived when he could make a contribution even greater than that of the two family predecessors he most admired: John Churchill, first Duke of Marlborough (1650–1722), and his own father Lord Randolph Churchill. David Cannadine has explored the doubtful benefit of this family legacy, from the alleged disloyalty of Marlborough's betrayal of James II and the 'unscrupulous and single-minded ardour' of his pursuit of power and riches, across generations of unstable inhabitants of Blenheim Palace, the Marlboroughs' stately home,

John Churchill, 1st Duke of Marlborough (1650–1722)
Sir Godfrey Kneller, c.1706
Oil on canvas, 927 × 737mm (36½ × 29″)
National Portrait Gallery, London (NPG 902)

The Water Terraces at Blenheim Palace

Lord Randolph Churchill (1849–95)
Harry Furniss, 1880s–1900s
Pen and ink drawing, 181 × 76mm (7⅛ × 3″)
National Portrait Gallery, London (NPG 3559)

Jeanette, Lady Randolph Churchill (1854–1921)
Nadar (Gaspard Felix Tournachon), 1890s
Albumen print, 301 × 183mm (11⅞ × 7⅛″)
National Portrait Gallery, London (NPG P499)

Churchill was born at Blenheim Palace. He admired his ancestor, the first Duke of Marlborough, and his father, the Conservative politician Lord Randolph Churchill.

Lady Churchill described Graham Sutherland as a 'Wow', a family term expressing strong approval. The painter initially felt welcome at Chequers, but he found Churchill's curiosity as the portrait developed disturbing and prevented him from seeing it. Shown the painting on completion, Churchill told Lord Moran, 'I think it is malignant.' After the presentation by the Houses of Parliament, Lady Churchill put it in the attic, and later had it cut up and incinerated. The National Portrait Gallery has two of Sutherland's preparatory oil sketches for the head and a compositional drawing. The transparency from which the painting has been reproduced here has discoloured with age but it is one of the few surviving records of the work.

down to Lord Randolph's 'erratic and uncontrollable' temperament. Churchill was variously accused by his enemies of all these faults, and certainly the name Churchill was not a political or social advantage at the dawn of the twentieth century. Undaunted, Winston Churchill sought both to rehabilitate his ancestor and his father in his biographies of them, and to live a political life that would have pleased Lord Randolph, something he had singularly failed to do as a schoolboy.

The portrait destroyed

Churchill's sense of himself as a man of destiny demanded that he retain a positive image of himself well into old age. His need to do so was demonstrated by the episode of the portrait by Graham Sutherland (1903–80). The Houses of Parliament commissioned Sutherland to paint a portrait of Churchill to mark his eightieth birthday in 1954. This might be seen with hindsight to have been rather

a risky venture; Sutherland was no flatterer, not a Frank Salisbury (1874–1962) imbued with a patriotic sense of illustrating a heroic national saga. His 1949 portrait of the writer William Somerset Maugham (1874–1965) should have been a warning. Sutherland studied ageing flesh and skeletal posture as he would a piece of driftwood, dispassionately, as a natural object subject to the ravages of time and place. The presentation ceremony in Westminster Hall was filmed and Churchill's double-edged remark on accepting the portrait conveyed the scorn of a weekend painter of conventional taste: '. . . a remarkable example of modern art'. It is well known that the painting was taken to Churchill's home at Chartwell in Kent and later destroyed by command of Lady Churchill. Sir Winston loathed it, claiming that 'it makes me look half-witted which I ain't'. The problem was, presumably, that he came up against an image of himself as an old, worn man, battered by time and circumstances, no longer a political force, but a spent one, the bulldog of the 1940s now a frail geriatric.

In contrast, two wartime photographs show the vigour that his own self-image demanded he retain undimmed into old age. The first is by the society photographer Sir Cecil Beaton (1904–80), equally at home with real power and with royal symbolism, who

ABOVE LEFT **Winston Churchill**
Sir Cecil Beaton, 1940
Bromide print, 237 × 190mm (9⅜ × 7½")
National Portrait Gallery, London (NPG x40055)

ABOVE RIGHT **Winston Churchill**
Yousuf Karsh, 1941
Bromide print, 280 × 216mm (11 × 8½")
National Portrait Gallery, London (NPG P490 (17))

The photographs and cartoons shown here encapsulate the popular image of Churchill. Features recorded faithfully in press and portrait photographs became humorously exaggerated by Sir David Low, Vicky and others. Funny hats sitting precariously on his round head, vast cigars, bow ties, siren suits, all engagingly eccentric in official and press photographs, become cheery weapons in the cartoonist's propaganda war. Idiosyncratic personal detail is transformed into dynamic, humorous defiance.

Winston Churchill
Artist and date unknown
Cigarette card, 68 × 35mm (2⅝ × 1¼″)
National Portrait Gallery, London (NPG D2695)

BELOW **Winston Churchill** and **Adolf Hitler**
(1889–1945)
Sir David Low
Charcoal and chalk, 1020 × 690mm (40 × 27″)
Evening Standard

BELOW RIGHT **Old Low's Almanac;**
Prophecies for 1955, published in the
Manchester Guardian, 1954

photographed Churchill at his desk in his first days in office as Prime Minister. It is a very businesslike image of managerial competence, his resolute expression turned to us as we interrupt his work, smart in appearance, a well-chewed cigar the indicator of true Churchillian quality; or perhaps we are the first to arrive for a Cabinet meeting, to occupy one of the places prepared at the table; as in the famous cartoon by David Low (1891–1963), we too must roll up our sleeves and get on with the job of winning the war. The second is by the Canadian photographer Yousuf Karsh (1908–2002), also known as Karsh of Ottawa, who photographed Churchill in 1941. The National Portrait Gallery has three images from the sitting, all three in a pose evocative of formal portraiture over the ages, left hand on hip, right hand on top of his chair; in one of them, Churchill's expression is fierce and bad-tempered, while the others are warm, and, playing against the traditional pose, show him smiling.

A tradition of political cartoons

Churchill's attitude to political cartoons of himself was more relaxed: such ephemeral mockery was all in a day's work for a democratic politician, unlike the permanence of an oil painting, which would hang, unless other measures were taken, before the jury of time. Churchill's facial characteristics and distinctive accessories made the cartoonists' job straightforward. He had a thorough understanding

Sir Winston Churchill
Graham Sutherland, 1954
Oil on canvas, 432 × 305mm (17 × 12")
National Portrait Gallery, London (NPG 5332)

Albert Finney as Winston Churchill
Played by Simon Ward in *Young Winston* (1971),
Churchill was villainously portrayed in several
Nazi films, and affectionately by Albert Finney in
The Gathering Storm (BBC/HBO 2002). His earliest
newsreel appearance was in 1910.

OPPOSITE
Statesmen of World War I
Sir James Guthrie, c.1924–30
Oil on canvas, 3962 × 3353mm (156 × 132")
National Portrait Gallery, London (NPG 2463)

of all this, and wrote about it in an article that appeared in 1932: 'One of the most necessary features of a public man's equipment is some distinctive mark which everyone learns to look for and recognise. Disraeli's forelock, Mr Gladstone's collars, Lord Randolph Churchill's moustache, Mr Chamberlain's eyeglass, Mr Baldwin's pipe – these properties are of the greatest value.' He went on, 'I have never indulged in any of them . . .' and explained how, without thinking, he had once donned a minuscule hat and been photographed, giving the cartoonists their 'distinctive mark'. From then on, hats became his signifier for the cartoonists, and he added 'Why should I complain? Indeed, I think I will convert legend into reality by buying a new hat for the purpose.' He may never have done so, but by 1940 the material was all there: cigars, bow ties, hats and sticks and his 'pouting cherub' expression; the addition of wartime details such as gas masks, siren suits and the V sign completed the repertoire, producing a popular image of vigorous defiance, laced with humour and sufficient eccentricity to be noticeable, but not dysfunctional.

A walk with destiny

The National Portrait Gallery has a painting that illustrates very well the difficulty of discussing Churchill's image and reputation, and will serve well as our concluding image of him. After the First World War, the patriotic millionaire Sir Abe Bailey (1864–1940) commissioned three group portraits of the wartime leadership: the soldiers, sailors and statesmen of the Empire. While other artists gave the uniformed military prosaic treatment, Sir James Guthrie (1859–1930) pulled out the iconographic stops in his portrait of the politicians. The Winged Victory of Samothrace hovers over the statesmen gathered around the table, in poses carefully worked out beforehand by the painter (he had himself photographed in most of them); the lighting is dramatic, an essay in the expressive use of *chiaroscuro*; and one man at the table is caught in a diagonal shaft of light that highlights his forehead as he stares directly at us with an expression of utter resolution. It is Winston Churchill, the youngest member of the Liberal war cabinet from 1914 to 1915, brought back into Lloyd George's coalition as Minister of Munitions in 1917. Looking at this picture now, it seems possible that, to Guthrie as he painted the picture, Churchill represented the future of Britain and the Empire. This prophetic interpretation is romantically Churchillian: it defies objective assessment.

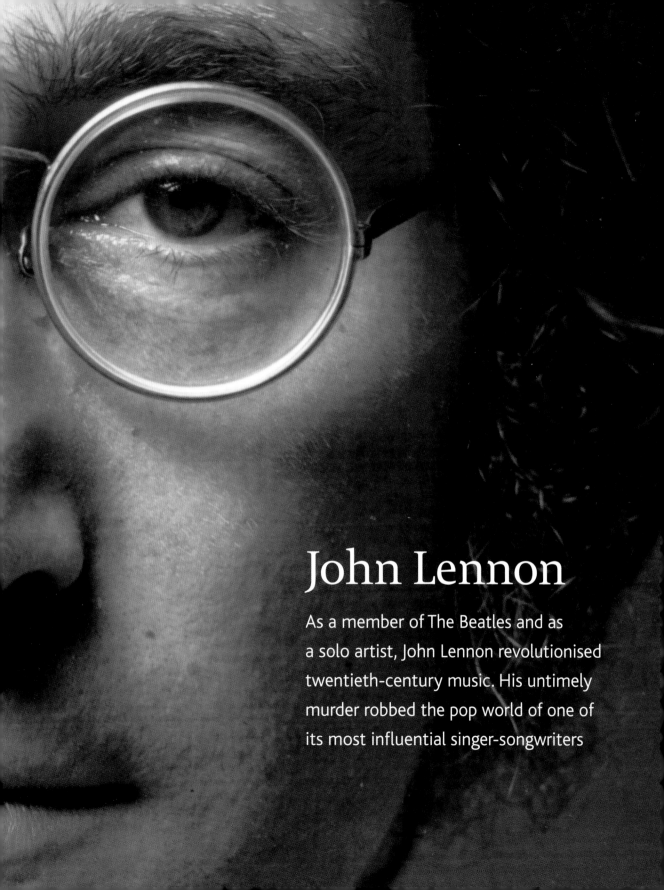

John Lennon

As a member of The Beatles and as
a solo artist, John Lennon revolutionised
twentieth-century music. His untimely
murder robbed the pop world of one of
its most influential singer-songwriters

'John . . . was driven by the need to question, to challenge, and to use himself as his own creative material'

Alan Davies, actor and comedian

In July 1980 John Lennon was sailing to Bermuda when his boat hit a storm. The rest of the crew were crippled with seasickness. It was John, who had hardly sailed before, who took the helm. He fought the waves for six hours until they reached safety.

It had been five years since he'd written a note of music. But there was something in this experience that inspired him. Perhaps it was his confrontation with the sea. Perhaps it was because he nearly died. Who knows, but he immediately began writing again. In less than six months he'd released a new album, *Double Fantasy*. And one month after that, in December 1980, he was shot dead.

When Mark Chapman pulled the trigger that killed the modern icon of idealism, hope and creativity, he was also firing a starting pistol for the hard, cynical, greedy 1980s. But Lennon had given the world a new way to think and that gunshot couldn't take it away. A chippy little lad from Liverpool had made himself immortal. How?

Maybe all greatness comes out of perfect historical encounters at perfect historical moments. When a teenager called Paul McCartney happened to find himself in the audience of a church fete concert in Liverpool on 6 July 1957, the conditions were certainly perfect. Rock and roll had caught the imagination of British youth: *Rock Around the Clock* had been playing in cinemas; the BBC had just started its first television chart programme; and Radio Luxembourg was playing Elvis Presley (1935–77) and Chuck Berry.

On the stage at the fete was John Lennon. He lacked technique, but he had an individual, raw energy. McCartney, who was more technically proficient, offered to show Lennon a few chords. Six years later, with the addition of George Harrison (1943–2002) and Ringo Starr, the choice of The Beatles as a band name, gigs in Hamburg and the

Cavern in Liverpool, and an encounter with a record-shop owner turned manager called Brian Epstein (1934–67), they had their first number one.

'Please Please Me' went to number one in March 1963 – the year the 1960s really began. Just another six years and The Beatles were no more – six years in which youth culture was born and came of age. Six extraordinary years of war, assassinations, protests and sexual revolution. The Beatles were at the heart of it all and Lennon at the heart of The Beatles. As a new generation tried to break free of the social straitjacket of the post-war years, it needed a voice. Lennon – who was going through the experience as profoundly as anyone – provided it.

John never saw himself as a leader: in fact he despised the very notion. But he was driven by the need to question, to challenge, and to use himself as his own creative material. He introduced to popular music a degree of personal exploration that was unprecedented. Once The Beatles had split, Lennon's raw openness expressed itself even more strongly in his albums *The Plastic Ono Band* and *Imagine*.

John Lennon was born the son of a seaman, Fred, and a cinema attendant, Julie. Fred went back to sea and Julie met another man. John was sent to be brought up by his aunt, Mimi. When he was five years old, his father returned, and his parents asked him to choose who he wanted to live with. He first chose his dad, then his mum. His mum sent him back to Mimi. His dad went back to sea. It wasn't until his teenage years that John formed a strong relationship with his mother. She encouraged him in his love of music, and bought him his first guitar. Then she was knocked down by a car and killed. As John later said, he lost his mother twice, once as a toddler and again when he was seventeen.

Everybody has pain in their lives, but John shared his with us in his music. Maybe that's why we feel such a strong

John Lennon 1940–80

9 October 1940	Born in Liverpool, the son of a merchant seaman, John is brought up by his Aunt Mimi and Uncle George but remains close to his mother
1956	Creates his first group, The Quarry Men: John meets Paul McCartney and George Harrison (1943–2002) whilst performing and they later join Pete Best and Stuart Sutcliffe(1940–62) to form The Beatles
1961	The Beatles first performance at the Cavern Club; Stuart Sutcliffe leaves the band and Brian Epstein becomes their manager
1962	Pete Best leaves the band and is replaced by Ringo Starr. Record deal with Parlophone. John marries Cynthia Powell in August
January 1963	'Please Please Me' goes to No.1 and a stream of hit records follows: 'I Wanna Hold Your Hand', 'Twist and Shout', 'She Loves You'. . . John's first son, Julian, is born in April
1965	The Beatles are named MBEs – four years later, John sends his back as a protest against Vietnam and Britain's involvement in Biafra and Nigeria
1966	Meets Yoko Ono at an art gallery; John later divorces Cynthia and marries Yoko in 1969
1971	Band members become increasingly distanced, eventually separating in a high court settlement
Early 1970s	Experiments with politics and appears on television talk show circuit. Releases first solo album, *Imagine* – the most commercially successful and critically acclaimed of all his post-Beatles efforts
1972	Organises charity concert in Madison Square Garden to help improve the living conditions of mentally handicapped children. John and Yoko perform at a series of rock concerts to spotlight various issues
9 October 1975	Second son, Sean, is born and John puts his music career on hold. Returns to career in 1980 with the album *Milk and Honey*
8 December 1980	Aged forty, John Lennon is murdered outside his New York apartment building, receiving multiple bullet wounds in his back

connection with him: we can relate to his vulnerability. The British are supposed to be an uptight lot. But we also have a strong streak of softness and sensitivity – we just get embarrassed about showing it. People like John Lennon help us find an outlet for it, through music – just like a great poet does through poetry. But the difference is that rock and roll is a loud, public expression. When John sang his pain out loud, he was singing a bit of ours for us too. He happened also to have the genius to write with a beauty and directness that would make his songs memorable to millions of people for decades to come.

The songs he wrote in Bermuda after his escape from the storm were about domestic life and happiness. Lennon was forty, and after a turbulent time he had settled down with Yoko Ono and their young son, Sean. John coined the term 'househusband' to describe the five years he spent bringing up Sean. Now he was back to music again.

In September 1980, he gave an interview to *Playboy* magazine. In it he said: 'Mahatma Gandhi and Martin Luther King are great examples of fantastic non-violents who died violently. I can never work that out. We're pacifists, but I'm not sure what it means when you're a pacifist and you get shot. I can never understand that.' In December, he was returning home from a studio in New York, and a fan shot him dead.

Lennon was a very ordinary Briton who was loved all over the world, and still is today. He's loved because he spoke for anyone who's ever suffered; because he spoke to anyone who's ever protested, or tried to bring about change; because he never tried to be a leader or to claim he was special; because he always expressed hope. And because he really did believe in peace.

By the time he died, he had made himself immortal because he'd been speaking in a language everyone could understand. 'Pop music is the people's form,' he said. 'Intellectuals trying to communicate with the people usually fail. Forget all the intellectual garbage, all the ritual of feeling – and express it in a sort of simple language that reaches people. No bullshit. If I want to communicate, I should use their language. Pop songs are that language.'

The image of a pop star

'Sexual intercourse began
In nineteen sixty-three
(Which was rather late for me) –
Between the end of the Chatterley ban
And the Beatles' first LP.'

PHILIP LARKIN (1922–85), *Annus Mirabilis*, 1974

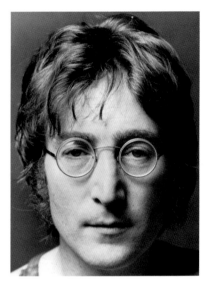

John Lennon
Iain MacMillan, 1971

Photographs of John Lennon at Quarry Bank High School show the incipient rocker challenging the school uniform code. At Liverpool College of Art this style developed, scruffily, until he fell in love with the twin-set wearing Cynthia Powell. John started appearing, briefly, in tweed jacket and flannels, a tribute to his love for Cynthia and evidence of his malleability in the hands of strong women. As The Beatles disintegrated, Yoko Ono's influence became paramount. John acknowledged her as his mentor in life and artistic expression. When first together, John echoed her face-framing hair and black-and-white clothes.

The classroom shook as the girls danced to the pulsating beat, yelling out the words, and giving a great 'Wooooo!' at the end. The patrolling headmistress was angry; she allowed the girls to stay in during wet dinner times and to play records, preferably serious music, although she was broadminded enough to permit 'hit parade' material; but this was too much. It had been going on all year, too, since that 'Love Me Do' nonsense before Christmas, then 'Please, Please Me' last term – the words were most unsuitable – and now a new one, and a long player too.

She stood on the platform at assembly to make her point, to defend the values and the ethos of the school against this distracting, corrupting influence. She made a little speech, condemning the music as crude, the words as suggestive, and the attitude of the singers as loutish and disrespectful. Then she broke the record over her knee.

That incident took place at a Liverpool girls' grammar school in May 1963, a school very near to Quarry Bank High, where the addictive sound and disrespectful attitude had originated in the late 1950s, its midwife one John Winston Lennon, leader of The Quarry Men, metamorphosing into Johnny and the Moondogs, The Silver Beatles, and finally The Beatles.

The restless chameleon

John Lennon made millions, but that was not the point. The point was to grow, the search a quest for his essential being. By the time of his death in December 1980, he seemed to have reached a kind of serenity, certainly a new plateau on the way up the mountain of self-discovery. Having completed his five self-imposed years of house-husbandry and child-rearing in accordance with his commitment, he had returned to the recording studio with Yoko Ono (1933–) to make their joint album *Double Fantasy*. After surviving an earlier fifteen-month separation, their mutual love, a creative and emotional union,

CLOCKWISE FROM TOP LEFT

Fan's photograph of John Lennon taken outside his
Aunt Mimi's house, 251 Menlove Avenue, Liverpool
Anne Fordham (aged 15), 1963

John Lennon
Astrid Kirchherr, c.1960
Photograph
Redferns Music Picture Library

Peter Best, George Harrison, John Lennon and
Paul McCartney in the dressing room of
The Cavern, Liverpool
Michael McCartney, early 1960s
Bromide print, 266 × 263mm (10½ × 10⅜")
National Portrait Gallery, London (NPG x88777)

John Lennon formed The Quarry Men in May 1957;
Paul McCartney joined later that summer and
George Harrison in February 1958. They became
The Beatles in June 1960.

had been unshaken since the birth of their son Sean five years
previously. John's music, always a refracted commentary on his state
of mind, now expressed the contentment and domesticity of life at his
and Yoko's apartment at the Dakota building overlooking New York's
Central Park. Was that going to be it? We shall never know, but it seems
unlikely that such a restless spirit would have ceased its searching.

Yoko Ono was not the only person to describe Lennon as a
chameleon. His adaptations to local colour and particular influences
were more than style decisions or the natural experimentation
of a secure adolescent trying things on; they were deeper-seated
expressions of an uncertain personal identity. Much has been written
about the difficulties of his early years, of how, as a 5-year-old, he
was asked to choose between his mother and his father, and of how
his mother gave him up to her sister, the redoubtable Aunt Mimi.
Witty, imaginative and energetic, he developed a carapace of truculent

Paul McCartney; John Lennon
20 Forthlin Road, Allerton, Liverpool (now owned by
the National Trust)
Michael McCartney, early 1960s
Bromide print, 255 × 254mm (10 × 10″)
National Portrait Gallery, London (NPG x88780)

John and Paul composed extensively together at
Paul's house. John lived mainly at his Aunt Mimi's,
occasionally in bed-sits.

The Beatles in Suits (George Harrison; Paul McCartney;
Ringo Starr; John Lennon)
Harry Hammond, 1963
Bromide print, 365 × 302mm (14⅜ × 11⅞″)
National Portrait Gallery, London (NPG x15550)

Brian Epstein built on Astrid Kirchherr's influence,
insisting on suits and ties as part of his shrewd
presentation of The Beatles as clean and safe, as
compared to the Rolling Stones.

toughness to see him through. A stranger to the conventional
requirements of the grammar school, he found his first identity and
an outlet for his energies in rock and roll. He adopted the persona of
a teddy boy: greased hair with a quiff, long jacket, tight black trousers
and brothel creepers. He formed a skiffle group at Quarry Bank High,
and began to perform at school and other local events. To the other
boys it was an amusement; to John it was his passion. Even to the
young Paul McCartney (1942–), then a pupil at the Liverpool Institute,
checking out The Quarry Men on 6 July 1957 at the St Peter's Woolton
church fete, music was only a hobby. 'I was a fat schoolboy,' reminisced
Paul about that first meeting, 'and as he leaned an arm on my
shoulder, I realised he was drunk.' McCartney, signed up for Boy
Scout camp, could not join John's group straight away. His father
saw the danger and warned him, 'Be careful of that John Lennon.
He could get you into trouble.'

Working hard at his image

At the Liverpool College of Art, John worked hard on his rock-and-roll,
tough-guy image. His caustic wit and anarchic attitude attracted
a coterie of friends and supporters; within this group he formed
a number of close friendships and had his first love affairs. His
biographers have rightly analysed his friendships at this time for
what they reveal about him. His survival at the college was almost
entirely due to the support of his teacher, Arthur Ballard, who,
recognising a rare quality of personal spirit and creative imagination
in the young man, argued for letting him stay when others wanted
him out. In John's favour, too, was his affinity with Stuart Sutcliffe
(1940–62), one of the most promising and dedicated students at the
college. Girls found John dangerously attractive, to the despair of their
mothers, and none more so than Cynthia Powell from respectable
Hoylake, near Birkenhead. The depth of John's fondness for Cynthia
can be gauged from his change of image; he modified his challenging
dress, and began to appear in flannel trousers and an old tweed
jacket of his Uncle George's, much more the look of a normal late-
1950s student. Cynthia, to some extent, refined him: he found in
her sense, efficiency and stability, some balm for his raw soul.

Another woman was responsible for a more significant change
in John's and the other Beatles' public image. On their first trip
to Hamburg in the late summer of 1960, they met the student

The Lennon Family
Cynthia, Julian and John Lennon
Robert Whitaker, 1965
Cibachrome print, 516 × 409mm (20¼ × 16")
National Portrait Gallery, London (NPG P732)

John Lennon met Cynthia Powell at the Liverpool
College of Art. An attraction of opposites, her calm
personality balanced his raw energy. Their marriage
was problematic to Brian Epstein, anxious about a
teenage idol appearing as a family man. Cynthia
remained at home with Julian, while John played the
lad on the road. The inevitable disrupted pattern of
the marriage was made worse by Cynthia's strong
disapproval of John's experiments with drugs. Then,
in September 1966, John met Yoko Ono: she offered
him an avant-garde adventure, a stimulating creative
mental and physical partnership beyond The Beatles
and Cynthia.

photographer Astrid Kirchherr. She became, in effect, their first
stylist. Accustomed to cutting her then boyfriend's hair by combing
it forward rather than back, and shaping it to the head, she persuaded
Stuart Sutcliffe, who was playing in the band at the time, to submit
to her scissors. John scoffed, a typical immediate reaction, but after
Paul and George Harrison (1943–2002) also agreed, he fell into line.
Only the drummer, Pete Best, kept his quiff. (Best was replaced by
Ringo Starr in August 1962.) The same happened with clothing:
Astrid had designed a collarless jacket, and John, who hated to be
led, or perhaps hated to recognise that he sometimes needed to
be led, was the last to adopt it. After Brian Epstein (1934–67) took
over the management of The Beatles in 1961, he was very strict
about smartening them up, so that as few people as possible would
be alienated by their appearance. John, again, went along with this
because the others agreed, and he saw the commercial rationale.
It went against the grain for him, though, and whenever he could,
he undid his top button and loosened his tie.

Artist and muse

The next sophisticated artistic woman to have a significant influence on John Lennon was Yoko Ono, whom he first met in November 1966. John was very candid and generous about the influence that Yoko had on him. For example, in an interview for *Playboy*, given in the year he died, he gave her full credit for shaping his mental life. He left the Beatles era behind, all the 'garbage' associated with it, because 'she's the teacher and I'm the pupil. She was there when I was nowhere, when I was the *nowhere man* . . .'. He also acknowledged the wisdom of her drastic action in throwing him out for fifteen months: 'Well, it was like being sent into the desert. And the reason she wouldn't let me back in was because I wasn't *ready* to come back in yet. And when I was ready to come back in, she let me back in. And that's what I am living with.' Yoko said herself that she was another Aunt Mimi for John, another strong, loving, controlling woman who provided stability and direction for a potentially wayward force.

John's appearance was changed by meeting Yoko, as one would expect. Yoko favoured black or white clothes, and her long black hair was an important part of her image. John, ever the chameleon, began to resemble her, growing his hair and adopting her colours; the white suit of the famous *Abbey Road* cover photograph dates from this period. He also replaced his second name, Winston, by Ono. It was all very

Left to right: Eamonn Andrews, John Lennon and Yoko Ono on the *Today* programme, 1969

John Lennon and Yoko Ono were married in Gibraltar on 20 March 1969. After lunching with Salvador Dalí in Paris, they moved on to Room 902 of the Amsterdam Hilton for their first 'bed-in' for peace, giving hundreds of interviews during the seven days. Pausing only to launch their film *Rape* in Vienna by giving a press conference from within a white bag, they arrived in London to appear on Thames Television's *Today* programme, inviting presenter Eamonn Andrews to join them in bed. Andrews was a popular TV personality; his conventional persona made him a good foil for John and Yoko.

hard for the ordinary Beatle fans to take: here was the rough, tough
leader of the group, the rasping rocker of 'Twist And Shout', coming
over all arty with a weird little foreign lady, making strange musical
sounds and appearing stark naked on the album cover of *Unfinished
Music no 1: Two Virgins*. And coming over all political too, with the
honeymoon bed-ins for peace at the Amsterdam Hilton, and at the
Queen Elizabeth Hotel in Montreal where they recorded 'Give Peace
A Chance'. John and Yoko's life became a mobile, high-profile,
worldwide, avant-garde art centre and political protest movement.
In November 1969, their recording label, Apple, issued John and
Yoko's *Wedding Album*, with a copy of their marriage certificate and
a photograph of a piece of wedding cake. In December, in eleven
cities worldwide, massive posters went up announcing: 'War is Over!
If You Want It. Happy Christmas from John and Yoko.'

Closing the door on 'the Fab Four'

Both this visible activity and the earnest sincerity behind it detached
John Lennon's identity from The Beatles, which he had in any case
always seen as a temporary phenomenon. In collaboration with
Yoko, he dared to break out and in doing so became a world figure

John Lennon
Harry Goodwin, *c.*1980

'Give Peace a Chance' was recorded on 1 June 1969, in John and Yoko's bedroom at the Queen Elizabeth Hotel, Montreal. It became the international anthem of the peace movement.

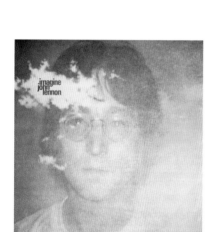

The sleeve design for the album *Imagine*, 1971.

and a hero of the counter-culture, particularly in the United States for his opposition to the Vietnam War. His post-Beatles music was an odyssey of self-discovery, from the political sloganeering of *Some Time in New York City* to the contentment of *Double Fantasy*. Some of it was raw, resonant with therapeutic cadences, suffused with the driving force of his restless psyche. It was the product of a life lived in search of himself.

The contrast with the pattern of Paul McCartney's life could not be more marked: Paul accepting his knighthood; John returning his MBE in protest against the Vietnam War. McCartney has, within the limitations imposed by being one of the most famous people in the world, lived a conventional life, based around strong family values, hard work at his chosen profession and astute management of all his resources, from cash to reputation. The 'fat schoolboy' showed all these qualities in embryo from the day he joined the band. Fully grounded, highly intelligent, good-looking, with a supernatural lyrical gift, he has acquired the great wealth and personal honour available to superb entertainers. Ever the diplomat (not a word you could use of Lennon), McCartney's political views and activities have never been allowed to shape his output as an entertainer. His music is the product of a natural musician's delight in being heard, drawing on his own experiences, but only so far as they enhance the music.

Give peace a chance

John Lennon and Diana, Princess of Wales, are commemorated in Havana, Cuba. Fidel Castro himself unveiled the life-size bronze statue of Lennon sitting on a bench, with words from 'Imagine' carved at his feet. There is a 'Parque John Lennon' and a 'Jardín Diana de Gales'. The author of a recent book on Havana was bewildered by 'the connection between a proudly socialist state and the most glamorous, media-hyped member of the British royal family', but found the Lennon memorial 'less anomalous', because the Cubans are ardent Beatles fans, despite the banning of their music from the mid-1960s until after they disbanded. This slightly misses the point. Surely they are there not because Diana was rich and royal, and Lennon was a Beatle, but for wider, humanitarian reasons: Diana because of her work for the sick and the damaged, Lennon because of his work for peace, and – because this is Cuba – for those elements of his songs and statements that could be interpreted as socialist.

John Lennon
Robert Whitaker, 1965
Cibachrome print, 306 × 408mm (12 × 16″)
National Portrait Gallery, London (NPG P734)

John's school friends waited eagerly for his satirical drawings of the teachers. At the Liverpool College of Art he did little, but impressed teacher Arthur Ballard with his originality. In 1970, under Yoko's influence he produced and exhibited a collection of lithographs, 'Bag One'; a vice squad raid ensured good sales. The collection is now in the Museum of Modern Art, New York. Much of his art was whimsical and humorous, and his later work such as the series 'Dakota Days', was suffused with love for Yoko and their son, Sean.

They are there too because of what we might loosely call their 'reach'; they transcended national boundaries and expressed our yearning for a better world. They provided an outlet for unfocused political and emotional protest at the perceived injustices of the systems of western liberal democracies.

John Lennon has many other memorials, from Central Park's 'Strawberry Field', opposite the Dakota building, to the airport at Liverpool. The World Wide Web is a major forum of commemoration, with sites dedicated to his personal achievement as well as to the whole Beatles phenomenon. Many of these sites feature quotations from other major figures of popular music testifying to the huge influence Lennon had on their ambitions. One site is dedicated to the Lennons of Liverpool, and gives biographies of John and his relations, tracing their ancestry back to Ireland. One US-based site has in-depth interviews with trusted associates, one of whom stresses

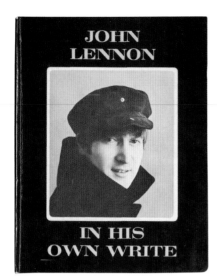

John Lennon: In His Own Write
(Jonathan Cape, 1964)

Both John Lennon's wives and their two sons
have been loyal to his memory and enhanced his
reputation. Yoko has been assiduous in supervising
reissues of his music and artwork. Cynthia robustly
attacked the muck-raking *The Lives of John Lennon*
by Arthur Goldman. Julian and Sean, as musicians,
have kept the flame burning.

OPPOSITE
John Lennon
Linda McCartney, 1968
Photograph, 514 × 356mm (20¼ × 14″)
National Portrait Gallery, London (NPG P575)

Paul McCartney and American photographer Linda
Eastman married in March 1969; no other Beatle
was invited to the wedding. Relations between Paul
and John worsened as the group disintegrated, with
Paul's affairs managed by Linda's family law firm.
Paul and John carried the dispute into music; John's
'How Do You Sleep?' was pure invective.

the warm feelings between Sean and Julian, Lennon's sons. Another
aspect of his posthumous identity as a radical hero is the reploughing
of the ground of his surveillance by the FBI following his application
for a Green Card. What seems like a sinister extension of that is the
inevitable theorising about the nature of his death, with some quite
serious people apparently convinced of a conspiracy to eliminate
him as a threat to 'Reagonomics'. In some quarters, he has to be
seen as a martyr.

Working-class hero

Let us return in conclusion to 1970, the year when The Beatles ended.
These were some of John's activities that year: he held an exhibition
of his lithographs, several of which were seized by the vice squad;
he and Yoko had their hair cut off, swapping it for Muhammad Ali's
boxing trunks; he paid the fines imposed on those protesting against
the visit of a South African rugby team; he revealed to a French
magazine that The Beatles smoked pot in the Buckingham Palace
lavatories in 1965; he and Yoko underwent primal scream therapy;
he ended a telephone message of support, broadcast to an 8,000-strong
CND rally in Victoria Park, Hackney, in London, by announcing that
Yoko was pregnant; he wrote and produced 'Instant Karma' in one
day and released it in ten; in December he released his first solo
album, *Plastic Ono Band*, showing the influence of Yoko and of the
raw exposure of his psyche resulting from the scream therapy.

All the passion, the indiscretion, the wacky stunts and sincere,
influential gestures are there, culminating in the release of an album
that took him deeply into himself, into the pain of the wound of
his upbringing that perhaps finally healed in his last five years. On
the album, the song 'Working Class Hero' was harsh and poignant,
described by his biographer Ray Coleman as 'a twentieth-century
folk song for Everyman'; a withering, scornful attack on a society
that suppresses the masses with cheap pleasures and religion.
The song is an outsider's anthem, a cry of pain from a wounded
but defiant young man, a social critique fuelled by personal misery.
In the song 'God', he rejected his own past, from Elvis to The Beatles,
but asserted the reality of his relationship with Yoko Ono. He was
his own and Yoko's man now.

Diana, Princess of Wales

Diana's fairy-tale wedding and subsequent divorce renewed interest in the state of the British monarchy. Her work for charity and her tragic death touched the hearts of the British public

'In her death she united an army of women and men in a sense of common purpose and belief'
Rosie Boycott, editor and journalist

When the news broke that Diana, Princess of Wales, had been killed in a car crash in Paris in 1997, the world reacted with a stunned silence, closely followed by overwhelming and almost universal grief. Why? Diana had never discovered or built anything, never won any wars, never written any plays or composed any music. Indeed, her critics would say she did nothing but tarnish the institution of the monarchy. And yet, in the days following her death, people came in their millions to pay homage to her memory. In her lifetime, Diana might not have headed an army, like Elizabeth I or Boudicca. Nevertheless in her death she united an army of women and men in a sense of common purpose and belief.

Diana's story, you see, is like a fairy tale – but not a Disney-style fairy tale with a happy ending. Real fairy tales are dark and full of warnings. This was to be a tale of innocence lost, and hope destroyed. Diana was the blonde princess who did not overcome adversity, and who never won the prince who would let her live happily ever after.

When the engagement between Prince Charles and Lady Diana Spencer was announced on 24 February 1981, there was rejoicing throughout Britain. For years, there had been high unemployment, race riots, strikes. Our monarchy was stuffy, insular and remote. Devoid of glamour, we needed a real princess. Here she was, a kindergarten teacher with a dull little page-boy haircut, innocent and pure. She made us feel protective. She was ours. Prince Charles, the most eligible bachelor of the 1970s, had picked out this Cinderella. Our dream had come true, and so, we thought, had hers.

But the Prince was not as pure as we all thought. Like the king in that other fairy tale, 'Bluebeard', he had one strict condition: his bride could share in his titles, land and riches, but there was one room into which she must never venture. For in that room was a secret; and the secret was called Camilla. Just a fortnight before the wedding, Diana

noticed a parcel in the Palace post room. Despite the protests of the Prince's staff, she opened it. Inside was a bracelet, and on it were engraved the letters G and F, entwined; Gladys and Fred – Charles and Camilla's nicknames.

Then came the day of the wedding. 'This is the stuff that fairy tales are made from,' the Archbishop intoned. We agreed, and Camilla looked on. What we didn't notice was that this Princess was already wasting away with anxiety. Between her first fitting for her wedding dress and the day of the wedding, Diana noted that her waist had shrunk from twenty-nine to twenty-three inches. She had already become bulimic.

Even on the honeymoon, Diana could feel Camilla's presence. As the newly-weds entertained the Egyptian President on the royal yacht *Britannia*, Diana noticed to her despair that Charles was wearing a new pair of cufflinks: on them were two Cs – entwined once more.

Within months, the cracks in the marriage began to appear. The joy of her first son William's birth faded fast. Diana grew thinner. Psychiatrists arrived at the palace. She was dying inside, from loneliness and a lack of love. She cut herself with razor blades and threw herself downstairs. In the background lurked Camilla – a secret the three of them shared, a secret like the blood on Bluebeard's key, that couldn't be washed away.

But as the House of Windsor froze in shock at the sight of their famous daughter-in-law falling apart, we just loved her more and more. Her charm, her beauty, her capacity to sit and hold hands with the old and sick and to talk about inconsequential things – these were far more potent than the disapproval of Buckingham Palace. By 1991, with the polls showing Diana to be the most popular member of the royal family, it was clear to everyone that the marriage was

Diana, Princess of Wales 1961–97

1 July 1961	Born to Frances and Edward John Spencer (later to become the 8th Earl Spencer)
November 1977	Prince Charles notices Diana at a shooting party at Althorp, the Spencer family estate in Northamptonshire; they start 'dating' in 1980
29 July 1981	Marries Prince Charles in St Paul's Cathedral. 600,000 people line the streets of London and millions watch the event on television
June 1982	Gives birth to Prince William – second in line to the throne after his father – and two years later Prince Henry or 'Harry' is born
July 1991	Whilst visiting a hospital, Diana hugs a sobbing AIDS patient and helps to dispel myths about the dangers of being near sufferers from the disease
June 1992	Andrew Morton's book, *Diana: Her True Story* is published. The book claims that Charles has had a long affair with Camilla Parker-Bowles, driving Diana to injure herself and attempt suicide
December 1992	Buckingham Palace announces the separation of the Prince and Princess of Wales
1994	Charles confesses to adultery during Jonathan Dimbleby's television documentary *Charles: The Private Man, The Public Role*. Dimbleby's biography *The Prince of Wales* details the affair with Camilla Parker-Bowles in 1972 and says that Charles married Diana to please his father
November 1995	Declares on the BBC's *Panorama* that she would like to be the 'queen of people's hearts' and admits that she was unfaithful to her husband with Captain James Hewitt
August 1996	Charles and Diana divorce: though still able to use the title 'Princess', Diana is no longer 'Her Royal Highness'
January 1997	Visits Angola to launch a campaign against landmines
June 1997	Christie's auction house in New York sells seventy-nine of Diana's gowns, raising $4.5 million for AIDS and cancer research projects
31 August 1997	Diana, her new companion Dodi Al-Fayed and their driver Henri Paul are killed in a high-speed car crash in a Paris tunnel

in trouble. Sure enough, in the autumn of 1992, Charles and Diana privately agreed to a separation.

The words 'stiff upper lip' could have been written for our royal family. The Windsors had always put a lid on their emotions: no tears at weddings, no tears at funerals. But Diana suddenly made this iciness look foolish. Her vulnerability became her greatest strength. And when she began to show that vulnerability, even in front of the television cameras, we didn't condemn her as weak or manipulative; we felt she was speaking the truth.

On 28 August 1996, Diana and Charles were finally divorced. Disowned by the royals, stripped of her title and privileges, Diana set out on a new quest: she began striding through minefields dressed in khaki, demanding landmines be banned, with right on her side. How could she find a new Prince Charming? We had put her on such a pinnacle that no one could ever be good enough. When she turned to Dodi Al-Fayed, we felt this millionaire playboy just wasn't right for our Diana. We froze her in a kind of deeply flawed perfection; we asked the impossible. How could it have gone on? This fairy tale only had one possible ending.

We wept when she died because she had no one to save her. We wept because we suspected she'd been dealt a cruel hand. We wept because we all felt a connection. We felt the innate sadness of our modern world that holds out the promise of so much for so many, but in fact leaves us weeping in its ultimate loneliness.

So, why does this make her great? Diana didn't have great abilities. Yet she knew that we all yearn to be loved, that we yearn for a world where gentleness rules over aggression, and where power is a force for good. From her unique position, she showed us that things aren't always what they seem. She acted out the fairy tale for us and showed us that the casket of gold is worthless. We didn't like these truths, but who else has ever shown them to us with such stark clarity and who else has ever paid quite such a high price for doing so?

As we watched her coffin make its slow and stately way up the long aisle of Westminster Abbey, we thought all those things and we wept. Just for a moment, the shy young kindergarten teacher made us pause. Is that the finest form of greatness? In its very special and curious way, I think it is.

The image of a princess

'She was the people's Princess.'

THE RT HON. TONY BLAIR, Prime Minister, 1997

Lady Diana Spencer at the nursery where she worked, 1980

Julie Burchill called this 'the first iconic image of Diana'. Later photographs would reflect a more calculating understanding of the possibilities of the photo opportunity.

Prince Charles and Lady Diana Spencer's royal wedding, 1981

She was taller than her fiancé, so the engagement photo-call had to be carefully staged. The ring must be visible, the happiness manifest and so the future assured. Perhaps her vibrant blue suit was a mistake, too much like Mrs Thatcher (or, as one cruel commentator said, a stewardess for Air Bulgaria), but the images duly appeared in the press and on television, and were well enough received; a reasonable result for the royal officials in charge. Their control was limited, though, and there was not much they could do about the famous 'see-through skirt' picture taken at the nursery where Diana worked – the selection of which by picture editors can, in retrospect, be seen as an early indicator of her tabloid popularity.

The official look for a princess

Two further images appeared in the months before the wedding in 1981, both of them officially sanctioned and expressing the identity the Palace was providing for the young woman. The first, the photograph by Lord Snowdon, is, by the standards of Diana's later years, unremarkable. It is bland and charming, showing a well-groomed young woman, spared conventional prettiness by the dimensions and shape of her nose. The second was the portrait by Bryan Organ, the unveiling of which was a major event for the National Portrait Gallery. The portrait was commissioned by the Gallery's Director and Trustees, with the full approval of the Prince of Wales, who thereby also signalled approval of his own image by Organ, which had been unveiled the previous year. The portrait of Charles has several interesting iconographical quirks, but its essence is a studied informality. This informality was something the royal family had been working on for the previous decade, as can be seen in the 1969 BBC documentary showing them barbecuing, buying sweets and giggling at verbose dignitaries. Organ's portrait shows the Prince in a jumper, with a canvas chair outlining the princely posterior. Small wonder then

ABOVE LEFT **Diana, Princess of Wales**
© Snowdon, 1981
Cibachrome print, 508 × 406mm (20 × 16″)
National Portrait Gallery, London (NPG P218)

ABOVE RIGHT **Diana, Princess of Wales**
Terence Donovan, c.1986
Bromide print, 301 × 203mm (11⅞ × 8″)
National Portrait Gallery, London (NPG P716(2))

These two photographs illustrate the transformation in Diana's appearance from newly engaged teenager to sophisticated Princess. Lord Snowdon has caught the freshness and naturalness of her early image; although recently divorced from Princess Margaret he was still favoured with family commissions. Diana became very fond of the bantering Terence Donovan, who once coaxed a smile from her by pulling a wad of notes from his back pocket and asking 'Recognise any of yer rellies [relations], love?' Donovan's photograph shows the effects of expensive grooming and the greater definition of her face caused by the slimming effects of bulimia and the strain of an unhappy marriage. During these years, Diana developed her understanding of the power of both portrait and press photographers, and learned to collude successfully with both.

that Diana should be depicted elegantly betrousered, cross-legged, mildly abusing the formality of a gilded chair. As in Snowdon's photograph, her face is bland, well-fleshed, giving little away, perhaps because at that stage there was nothing to give.

There are compositional similarities between the two Organ portraits that are part of the story they tell, and that have a singular poignancy in Diana's case. Charles is placed against a large fence, as looming a structural element as Brunel's chains, topped by a Union flag, the whole jokily symbolic of the burden he must one day bear as monarch. Diana, informal in her body language, is framed against, even defined within, the rigid geometry of the door and tall skirting board in the Chinese Drawing Room at Buckingham Palace. Ah, we all said, that's why she's there, an officially sanctioned breath of fresh air, bringing youth and natural informality into the right angles of their lives. Older and sadder, but probably none the wiser, we later came to see that the frame became an impossible constraint.

As Diana's marriage deteriorated in the mid-1980s and she suffered the wasting effects of chronic bulimia, she continued to fulfil her joint roles as royal mother and cover girl. The roles were

complementary: images of idyllic young motherhood filled those spaces not already given over to her solo appearances. This was not a new phenomenon; images of fecund young women, the brood mares of the blood line, are essential for a hereditary monarchy. If these young women are also beautiful, further benefits accrue in terms of wide exposure leading to positive familiarity. We can see the process beginning with Princess Alexandra of Denmark (1844–1925), later Queen Consort of Edward VII (1841–1910), who came on the scene as mass-market photography was invented in the form of *cartes-de-visite*; she appeared in thousands of reproductions, either alone or with her children; another beauty, the late Queen Mother (1900–2002), had similar exposure, as did Queen Elizabeth II, whose beauty as a young woman has been frequently recalled during her Jubilee year.

In 1992 Diana confirmed, through the medium of the bestselling book by Andrew Morton, many of the rumours and stories about her failing marriage, and the struggle within the confines of the royal family that had driven her to illness and attempted suicide. Morton relates that she decided to take control of her life, and that her capacity to do so was boosted by finding that she could cope with tragedy and its aftermath; in particular the death of one of the royal party in a skiing accident in March 1988. By controlling herself,

ABOVE LEFT **Prince Charles** (b.1948)
Bryan Organ, 1980
Acrylic on canvas, 1778 × 1782mm (70 × 70⅛″)
National Portrait Gallery, London (NPG 5365)

ABOVE RIGHT **Diana, Princess of Wales**
Bryan Organ, 1981
Acrylic on canvas, 1778 × 1270mm (70 × 50″)
National Portrait Gallery, London (NPG 5408)

In different circumstances she would have grown older and more regal, the subject of dozens of dignified, official portrait paintings. The National Portrait Gallery would have collected a series of canvases milestoning her advancing years, as with Queen Elizabeth, the Queen Mother. Bryan Organ's portrait stands alone, and now seems to symbolise the world from which she escaped, the tight frame of the background prophetically constricting. Photography and video were her media: instantaneous, accessible, demotic, reflecting the beauty, conferring the glamour, often importunate and disrespectful, but conveying her messages and defining her memorial.

BELOW LEFT **Elizabeth II and Princess Anne**
Marcus Adams, c.1951
Bromide print, 286 × 228mm (11¼ × 9")
National Portrait Gallery, London (NPG P140(24))

BELOW RIGHT **Diana with her two sons, Princes William and Harry**
John Swannell, 1994
Iris print, 394 × 482mm (15½ × 19")
National Portrait Gallery, London (NPG P717(16))

During her marriage Diana found it hard to reconcile the demands of her royal duties with the spontaneous giving of maternal love. The Windsors' concept of monarchical duty has not permitted them to develop a child-centred view of upbringing. Diana's own family was similar, and she was determined to provide warmth, stability, and normal fun for her boys to balance the country sports encouraged by their father. Some expressed surprise that they were permitted to wear baseball caps, eat hamburgers and visit theme parks, and there was much tut-tutting when she took them, under-age, to a certificate 15 film.

managing the practicalities, condoling with the bereaved, and in the process winning several disputes with her husband, Diana, to put it in her terms, began a process of personal renewal. David Bailey's photograph, taken later that year, embodies the new attitude (page 160). It is an image of great sophistication, the artificial informality of the Organ portrait replaced by what appears to be the genuine article, classy, warm and exuding the humorous, seductive charm for which she was to become increasingly celebrated.

By this time, too, she was well on the way to becoming, as the writer Salman Rushdie put it, 'a master semiotician', meaning by this that she understood the language of visual messages. She may not have had any significant book learning, but she was adept at manipulating, and communicating through, images. 'Thicky Spencer' she may have been at school, but by the time she died she was a master at managing both still and moving images, and of the knowledge that 'image' means a total package of public (re)presentation. In an interview with Tina Brown for the *New Yorker* just before she died,

Diana, Princess of Wales
David Bailey, 1988
Bromide print, 504 × 373mm (19⅞ × 14¾")
National Portrait Gallery, London (NPG P397)

Diana, Princess of Wales
Terence Donovan, c.1990
Bromide print, 306 × 201mm (12 × 7⅞")
National Portrait Gallery, London (NPG P716(11))

The Sloane Ranger gave way to the outwardly confident, glamorous, funny, flirtatious, media-savvy celebrity.

Diana explained how she had tried to persuade the Palace to take on a media adviser, to reposition the monarchy for the television age she understood so well. 'They kept saying I was manipulative,' complained Diana, 'but what's the alternative? To just sit there and have them make your image for you?'

Press victim or manipulator?

How far did Diana control the development of her image? Let us look briefly at these areas: portrait photographs; press and television images; and the spoken word. (We have already seen examples of how she made use of the printed word.) Collaborative and symbiotic seem appropriate descriptions of the relationship between Diana and the portrait makers; her looks and social position, as both a fully paid-up royal and a defiant celebrity outcast, made her an intriguing subject and a prize catch. It was in Diana's interests to present herself as healthy, beautiful, in control, and living a life beyond the Windsors. The French photographer Patrick Demarchelier took a series of pictures for the Morton book, and he is described in the book as 'Diana's favourite photographer'. Set against a plain background, these photographs emphasise, without distraction, Diana's physical elegance and mature beauty, and in several of them her hands are positioned to display her wedding ring, a piquant detail in retrospect. One further detail: the acknowledgements in Morton's book state that Demarchelier donated his fee to the charity Turning Point. Without sneering at his generosity, we can discern here another element of Diana's image in the making, her association with the fusion of altruism and image-massaging that characterises much charity work at the glossier levels of society.

Mario Testino was commissioned to photograph Diana for *Vanity Fair* in 1997, and these images were again seen in his major retrospective at the National Portrait Gallery in 2002. Testino, like all successful portrait photographers, has the ability to relax his celebrated subjects and achieve results that are both glamorous and accessible. The record-breaking success of the exhibition confirmed Testino's ability to satisfy, in his case at a high aesthetic level, the demand for images of high-powered celebrity; here at least it seems that Diana has achieved a kind of immortality, her image hermetically sealed against the greasy fingers of posterity (see pages 152-3).

Diana collaborated closely with Demarchelier, Testino, Terence

Diana: Her True Story – In Her Own Words
Book jacket of Andrew Morton's biography of
Diana (Michael O'Mara Books, 1992)

Today newspaper, 1995 following Diana's decision
to appear on *Panorama*

Diana photographed alone at the Taj Mahal
during the India Tour, 1992

After a hectic introduction to the demands of the
media, and, according to her, little guidance from
the Palace, she learned to use the system to her
own advantage. She cultivated favourable journalists,
joshed with photographers, and posed obligingly.
As marital war broke out she skirmished dexterously,
providing newsworthy images more eloquent than
columns of print. She gave those too, via Andrew
Morton's tape recorder, and declared open war via
prime-time television.

Donovan and all the other celebrity photographers, enjoying their
skill and happy in their social circle. With press photographers, on
the other hand, and to some extent TV news crews and their editorial
bosses, there were difficulties. She could not control them; only, like
any media-savvy celebrity, submit to them with good grace on most
occasions, and learn how to work photo-opportunities around to her
advantage. While still a young Sloane, she showed good-humoured

aplomb when pursued to her car by the rat pack. Ten years later, she was bold enough, even desperate enough, to provide evidence of her decaying marriage by posing emphatically alone for the press corps in front of the Taj Mahal, built as a symbol of unsullied marital bliss, during what was supposed to be a joint tour of India with her husband. Two days later, the press received further confirmation from Diana of her bleak situation: dragooned into presenting the prizes at a polo match, she stood up to do her duty; then, finding that one of the recipients was her husband and that he was leaning forward to give a thank-you kiss, she moved her cheek away at the moment the shutters clicked. Hardly subtle exercises, but highly effective in communicating her message to the world – and to the *whole* world at that – and, in using an official occasion to express private feelings, about as un-Windsorish an approach as she could have conceived. Her fusion of the private and personal with the public function of royalty was a complete and deliberate denial of the separation of the human body and its emotions from royal being that is essential to the Windsors' interpretation of their role. In traditional monarchical philosophy, the person of the monarch is separate from their royal dignity: the Windsors may appear stiff and formal, but much of this is caused by their strict interpretation of what constitutes appropriate behaviour.

Her human touch

As Richard Coles, the writer, musician and broadcaster, commented, Diana had 'that trick of embodying royalness and subverting it in your favour simultaneously [that] one of the surviving royals would do well to master'. He cited the occasion when a friend of his appro-priated the name badge of the Princess of Prussia who had left a function early, and wore it when introduced to Diana. 'There's only one princess around here, honey!' Diana said, and then plunged in, scattering charm, chatter and indiscretions about her relations. Countless other examples could be cited of similar subversive encounters. Often they were the prelude to more serious engage-ment, particularly if she was visiting sick or distressed people. Then her intuitive sympathy, fuelled by her own unhappy marital and earlier family experiences, brought direct comfort: this was the challenge to precedent, anathema to the Windsors' banishment of inner self from royal function.

Diana, Princess of Wales, in Angola with landmine victims, 1997

Diana's impulse to undertake charity work stemmed from her own natural inclinations, observable in her childhood, and from the identification with misery forced upon her by her family's break-up. Thrust into royal duties, she developed a new style of emotional communication, de-stigmatising the suffering of AIDS patients, the homeless and the battered. In her last year she helped the campaign against landmines, travelling to Angola and Bosnia under the auspices of the Red Cross. An experienced observer, a hard-bitten journalist with fifty years' experience of peace and war, commented on her skill in using touch rather than voice to offer comfort.

It is too early to tell what effect this will have on the monarchy's interpretation of its public role. There is some evidence that the Prince of Wales is going beyond the traditional Windsor boundaries of emotional expression. A cynical observer of the Queen Mother's funeral pointed out that Charles's display of grief, before, during and after, was a move in the Diana direction, and that, while doubtless sincere, it was a piece of emotional repositioning in the battle for the hearts and minds of his future subjects.

Diana watched a lot of television and understood its power both as a disseminator of information, and as a medium conferring authenticity on the message it delivered. Her *Panorama* appearance on 20 November 1995 made complete sense in this context, as the star of the nation's classiest soap opera gave her raw emotional wounds serious political significance. The Morton book, published three years earlier, had its origins in tabloid journalism, and although the tabloids were being increasingly proved right in their sensational allegations, the authority of *Panorama* inevitably carried greater weight. Diana spoke to the nation directly, not indirectly as in the book; the alleged 'basket case' struck back at 'my husband's department'. Defining herself as an ordinary person (intriguing, this, from a super-rich aristo-crat brought up on a royal estate – but some-how one knew what she

Diana, Princess of Wales, arriving at the opening of the exhibition *Richard Avedon: Evidence 1944–94* at the National Portrait Gallery, London

Photography and dance were the art forms with which Diana was most associated. Diana and the celebrity photographers had much to give each other; she was their subject, friend and patron. She had a working rapport with most of the regular press pack, but endured the intrusive *paparazzi*. She was a supporter of ballet, having been a good dancer as a girl, although too tall to take it further. She did make one famous appearance at Covent Garden, doing a routine with Wayne Sleep at a gala evening, to her husband's disapproval. Thereafter she maintained links with the English National Ballet, even after she withdrew from many other commitments.

The *Panorama* interview
Diana is interviewed by Martin Bashir in the
BBC documentary, 1995

The *Panorama* interview confirmed how far Diana
was from the public style and private feelings of her
husband's family. Its confessional, self-revelatory tone
was interpreted as an assertion of her independence.

IRREPLACEABLE

Fourth anniversary of the death of Diana, 2001
For Diana's funeral, Buckingham, Kensington and
St James's palaces were wreathed in flowers. The
route was extended from 1.6 to 4 kilometres to
accommodate the expected more than one million
mourners. Over a billion watched worldwide on
television.

OPPOSITE
Diana at the Hilton Hotel Humanitarian Awards,
New York, December 1995

meant in comparison with the Windsors), she described her bulimia,
confessed to adultery with the 'adored' James Hewitt, encouraged
the monarchy to be less distant with the people, and claimed she
was a 'free spirit' who knew she would never be queen, but aspired to
be a 'Queen of Hearts'. It was an extraordinary, reckless, courageous,
moving and sometimes embarrassing performance. 'I'm not a political
animal,' she asserted, but posterity will beg to differ. She was not
party political, perhaps, but in all other senses of the phrase she was a
formidable operator; in the *Panorama* interview, to quote Richard Coles
again, 'she exchanged her royalty for celebrity. In the place of duty,
reserve, mystery, she claimed openness, honesty, transparency.'

Not political, indeed? Her appearance at the Serpentine Gallery,
her workaday radiance enhanced by a glow of defiance, on the night
of the Prince of Wales's TV interview with Jonathan Dimbleby in
1995, was impeccably timed to catch the mid-evening news bulletins,
the breakfast transmissions and the morning papers, and has passed
into the legends of intra-marital strife. This was, as Julie Burchill has
put it, a classic example of the lemon in the honey; a calculated,
aggressive counter-move by an experienced schemer using all her
physical assets and media-savvy to put one over on the other side.
Her own constituency loved her for it: what style, chutzpah, class
and confidence – and what a dress!

A sense of belonging

If we need to justify Diana's presence amongst the Great Britons,
perhaps we need only look at how, in the courageous rebuilding of
her life after a disastrous marriage, she stumbled across and then
used with increasing confidence and effect an alternative pattern of
monarchical behaviour. Using her three salient characteristics of
personal beauty, emotional literacy and grasp of imagery, and with
the help of skilled professionals, she learned to appeal to a wide
constituency of the young, the disillusioned and the potentially
excluded, for whom the traditional expressions of both hereditary
and elective power had little appeal. While still officially royal, she
displayed a completeness in which whatever was 'royal' was mediated
through warm, personal contact, and in which she not only attempted
to dignify suffering, but also introduced a new dynamic of emotional
identification, conferring a sense of worth and belonging on those
whom she chose to favour with her unique brand of shy charm.

Epilogue: the great debate

The Great Britons poll provides an important touchstone for national opinion on the people that we currently admire. The results record what we value today in our history and culture: from ideas to action, heroism to compassion, artistic endeavour to scientific enquiry. It is anticipated that *Great Britons* will stimulate debate about what it means to be British. This is important because national identity can play a significant role in distinguishing and promoting our education, manufacturing and creative industries abroad.

A further element in this debate is the question, 'who will we consider 'great' in future? For example, the opportunities for many in our society to hold positions of power have been limited until the last fifty years and thus the list of 100 does not and cannot reflect the diversity of contemporary Britain.

It is our hope in publishing this book that it will encourage the public to consider our national self-image and that it will inspire a new generation to celebrate their mentors and heroes.

CELIA JOICEY
Publishing Manager,
National Portrait Gallery, London

Key for pie charts

Oliver Cromwell

William Shakespeare

Isambard Kingdom Brunel

Diana, Princess of Wales

John Lennon

Winston Churchill

Elizabeth I

Charles Darwin

Isaac Newton

Horatio Nelson

Books referenced on the British Library catalogue search engine

As a playwright, poet and author, Shakespeare has by far the most books listed on the British Library catalogue search engine, with 10,461 entries. Brunel has the least number of references, with sixty-five.

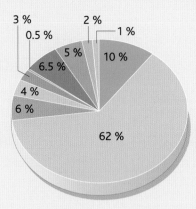

Films made on each subject listed on the International Movie Database

The most popular subject for film makers is Churchill, played by, amongst others, Bob Hoskins, Richard Burton and Albert Finney. There have been no feature films made about Brunel but in 1975 an animated short film by Bob Godfrey, *Great*, took an irreverent look at the engineer and won the Academy Award for Best Animated Short Film.

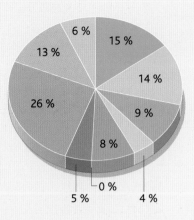

Portraits in the collections of the National Portrait Gallery, London

Portraits play a major part in defining our national self-image. There are more representations (thirty-seven) of Cromwell in the collections of the National Portrait Gallery than any other Great Briton. Brunel and Churchill have the least with ten portraits each.

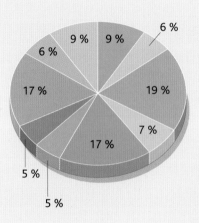

Sales of postcards

Arguably women help to sell merchandise better than men. National Portrait Gallery postcard sales of Elizabeth I during 2001 outstripped the total number of postcard sales for all the other men in the top ten. The least popular postcard subject in the top ten was Nelson.

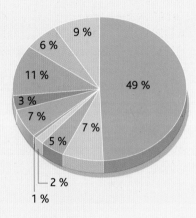

Website references on www.bbc.co.uk

Of all the Great Britons, Elizabeth I has the highest number of website references listed under a UK search. Unfortunately it is difficult to distinguish these from Elizabeth II website matches. Brunel has the lowest number of websites that reference him.

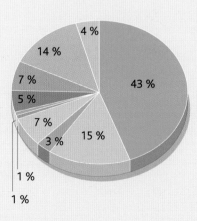

Number of streets named after each subject listed on www.streetmap.co.uk

Despite the difficulties of distinguishing between streets named after Elizabeth I or Elizabeth II, Newton is still the most popular subject when naming a road. Lennon has received relatively few similar tributes.

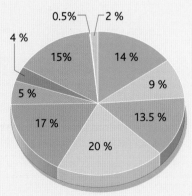

Bibliography

WILLIAM SHAKESPEARE

Edmond, Mary, *The Chandos Portrait: a suggested painter* (*Burlington Magazine*, Volume CXXIX, March 1982)

——, *'It was for gentle Shakespeare cut'* (*Shakespeare Quarterly*, Fall 1981)

Piper, D., *O Sweet Mr Shakespeare! I'll have his picture* (National Portrait Gallery, London, 1964)

Schoenbaum, S., *Shakespeare's Lives* (Oxford University Press, 1979)

Strong, Roy, *Tudor and Jacobean Portraits* (Her Majesty's Stationery Office, for National Portrait Gallery, London, 1969)

Taylor, Gary, *Reinventing Shakespeare* (Hogarth Press, London, 1990)

ELIZABETH I

Campbell, Lorne, *Renaissance Portraits* (Yale University Press, New Haven and London, 1990)

Rowse, A. L., *The Elizabethan Renaissance* (Macmillan, London, 1972)

Starkey, David, *Elizabeth* (Vintage, London, 2001)

Strong, Roy, *Tudor and Jacobean Portraits* (Her Majesty's Stationery Office, for National Portrait Gallery, London, 1969)

——, *Gloriana* (Thames and Hudson, London 1987)

OLIVER CROMWELL

Cooper, John, *Oliver the First: Contemporary Images of Oliver Cromwell* (National Portrait Gallery, London, 1999)

Coward, Barry, *Oliver Cromwell* (Longman, London 1994)

Fraser, Antonia, *Cromwell, Our Chief of Men* (Weidenfeld and Nicolson, London, 1973)

Hill, Christopher, *God's Englishman: Oliver Cromwell and the English Revolution* (Weidenfeld and Nicolson, London, 1970)

Morrill, John (ed.), *Oliver Cromwell and the English Revolution* (Longman, London, 1992)

Richardson, R. C. (ed), *Images of Oliver Cromwell* (Manchester University Press, 1993)

ISAAC NEWTON

Fara, Patricia, *Newton: the Making of a Genius* (Macmillan, London, 2002)

Jordanova, Ludmilla, *Defining Features: Scientific and Medical Portraits 1660–2000* (Reaktion Books, London, 2000)

Porter, Roy, *Enlightenment: Britain and the Creation of the Modern World* (Allen Lane/The Penguin Press, London, 2000)

Stewart, J. Douglas, *Sir Godfrey Kneller and the English Baroque Portrait* (Clarendon Press, Oxford, 1983)

Fauvel, John (et al.), *Let Newton be! A New Perspective on his Life and Works* (Oxford University Press, 1988)

HORATIO NELSON

Colley, Linda, *Britons: Forging the Nation 1707–1837* (Yale University Press, New Haven and London, 1992)

Fraser, Flora, *Beloved Emma: the Life of Emma Hamilton* (Papermac, London, 1999)

Hibbert, Christopher, *Nelson: a Personal History* (Viking, London, 1994)

Pocock, Tom, *Horatio Nelson* (Pimlico, London, 1994.)

Walker, Richard, *Nelson Portraits* (Royal Naval Museum, Portsmouth, 1998)

ISAMBARD KINGDOM BRUNEL

Buchanan, R. Angus, (et al) *Isambard Kingdom Brunel: Recent Works* (Design Museum, London, 2000)

Rolt, L.T.C., *Isambard Kingdom Brunel* (Longmans, Green, London, 1957)

——, *George and Robert Stephenson* (Longmans, Green, London, 1960)

Rogers, Malcolm, *Camera Portraits* (National Portrait Gallery, London, 1989)

Hamilton, Peter and Hargreaves, Roger, *The Beautiful and the Damned* (Lund Humphries, London, 2001)

CHARLES DARWIN

Hopper, K. Theodore, *The Mid-Victorian Generation 1846–1886* (Clarendon Press, Oxford, 1998)

Bowler, P. J., *Charles Darwin: the Man and His Influence* (Blackwell, Oxford, 1990)

Briggs, Asa, *The Age of Improvement* (Longmans, Green, London, 1959)

Desmond, Adrian and Moore, James, *Darwin: the Life of a Tormented Evolutionist* (Penguin Books, London, 1991)

Hull, D. L., *Darwin and His Critics* (University of Chicago Press, 1983)

WINSTON CHURCHILL

Blake, Robert and Louis, W. R., (eds) *Churchill* (Oxford University Press, 1993)

Churchill, Winston (Abridged by D. Kelly into one volume) *The Second World War* (Cassell, London, 1959)

Gilbert, Martin, *Churchill: A Life* (Pimlico, London, 2000)

Jenkins, Roy, *Churchill* (Pan Books, London, 2002)

Roberts, Andrew, *Eminent Churchillian* (Weidenfeld and Nicolson, London, 1994)

JOHN LENNON

Coleman, Ray, *Lennon* (Pan Books, London, 2000)

Davies, Hunter, *The Beatles* (Heinemann, London, 1968)

Lennon, Cynthia, *A Twist of Lennon* (W. H. Allen, London, 1978)

Sheff, David, *Last Interview* (Pan Books, London, 2001)

Turner, Steve, *A Hard Day's Write* (Carlton, London, 1994)

DIANA, PRINCESS OF WALES

Burchill, Julie, *Diana* (Weidenfeld and Nicolson, London, 1998)

Campbell, Beatrix, *Diana, Princess of Wales: How Sexual Politics Shook the Monarchy* (The Women's Press, London, 1998)

Dimbleby, Jonathan, *The Prince of Wales* (Little, Brown, London, 1994)

Merck, Mandy, (ed) *After Diana: Irreverent Elegies* (Verso, London, 1998)

Morton, Andrew, *Diana: Her True Story* (Michael O'Mara Books, London, 1992)

Picture credits

Every effort has been made to contact copyright holders; any omissions are inadvertent, and will be corrected in future editions if notification is given to the publisher in writing. We are grateful to the owners and the following copyright holders who have kindly agreed to make their images available in this catalogue:

© Derek Allen, p.12 (left)
Associated Press: p.146
© David Bailey: pp. 8, 155, 160 (top)
By kind permission of the Bank of England: pp.52 (bottom)
Courtesy of the Barbican Centre: p.52 (top)
© Birmingham Museums & Art Gallery: p.61
Bristol Tourism and Conference Bureau: p.106 (left and right)
Britannia Films Ltd/Majestic Films: p.48 (bottom)
© BBC Picture Archives: pp. 11 (left and right), 38 (top), 136 (bottom), 164 (bottom)
The British Library/Irene Rhoden: p.79 (left)
© Copyright The British Museum: p.78 (bottom)
© Hamish Brown, p.12 (right)
In the collection of the Duke of Buccleuch & Queensberry, KT: p.60
© Courtesy of Department of Plant Sciences, University of Cambridge: p.121 (right)
By permission of the Syndics of Cambridge University Library: pp.115 (left), 119 (top)
Terence Donovan/Camera Press: pp.157 (right), 160 (bottom)
Marcus Adams/Camera Press: p.159 (left)
C4 films/Polygram Filmed Entertainment /RGA: p.38

Christie's Images Ltd 1994: p.51
Christie's Images Ltd 2002: p.150
Photograph © Annie Leibovitz/Contact Press Images, courtesy of the artist: p.147 (right)
Copyright reserved: pp.18 (bottom), 66 (bottom), 129 (left), 143 (top left)
Salvador Dali/Gala-Salvador Dali Foundation/DACS 2002/Christie's Images Ltd 2001: p.80 (bottom)
Estate of Robert Elliot: p.128
Evening Standard/Atlantic Syndication: p.135 (bottom left)
Fitzwilliam Museum, Cambridge: p.77 (bottom left)
By permission of the Folger Shakespeare Library: p.49 (right)
© Harry Goodwin: p.148 (top)
© Harry Hammond: p.144 (bottom left)
© Estate of George Harcourt: p.131 (bottom)
© Roger Hargreaves: p.163
By kind permission of the Holy Trinity Church, Stratford-upon-Avon: p.46
© The Imperial War Museum, London: pp.25, 124–5, 131 (top)
© Courtesy Yousuf Karsh: cover (detail) pp.9, 127, 130, 134 (right)
© The Kobal Collection: p.85
Iain Macmillan/© YOKO ONO: cover (detail) pp.25, 138–9, 142
By kind permission of His Grace the Duke of Marlborough: p.132 (top right)
© Manchester Guardian/David Low: p.135 (bottom right)
Copyright Estate Linda McCartney: pp.8, 141, 151
© Michael McCartney: pp.143 (bottom left), 144 (top left)
Reproduction of 'An Interview between Charles I and Oliver Cromwell' by Daniel Maclise courtesy of the

National Gallery of Ireland: p.64
National Gallery, London, p.14 (right)
© National Maritime Museum, London: pp.87, 89 (top), 90 (bottom), 91 (bottom left and right)
© National Maritime Museum, London, Greenwich Hospital Collection: p.95
© National Museums & Galleries of Wales: p.32
Courtesy of the Board of Trustees of the National Museums and Galleries on Merseyside (Lady Lever Art Gallery, Port Sunlight): p.65 (left)
National Portrait Gallery, London: cover (details) pp.8, 9, 10, 13 (left), 14 (left and centre), 15, 19–21, 22 (left), 24, 25, 29, 30, 32 (bottom), 35, 37, 39, 43–5, 48 (top), 49 (left), 50 (bottom), 54–5, 57–8, 59 (left and right), 60 (top), 62, 63 (top and bottom), 66 (top), 67, 71, 75 (bottom), 76, 81, 82–3, 85, 86, 88, 89 (bottom), 90 (top), 91 (top), 92, 93, 94, 96–7, 99, 100, 101 (top left and right), 102–5, 107–9, 113, 116–8, 119 (bottom), 120, 121 (left), 123, 129
© Helen Curtis, National Trust: p.72
© The Natural History Museum, London: pp.25, 110–1, 114, 122 (left and right)
Photo by John and Yoko/© YOKO ONO, p.147 (left)
Photo Scala, Florence: p.33
By kind permission of the Trustees of the Portsmouth Estates: p.73
© Private Collection: p.77 (top)
By kind permission of the Provost, Fellows and Scholars of the Queen's College, Oxford: p.47
Astrid Kirchherr/Redferns: p.143 (right)
Rex Features: pp.156 (top and bottom), 161 (bottom right)

David Hartley/Rex Features: p.161 (left)
Nils Jorgensen/Rex Features p.164 (bottom)
Tim Rooke/Rex Features: pp.162, 165
© Royal Academy of Arts, London: p.65 (right)
From the RSC Collection with the Permission of the Governors of the Royal Shakespeare Company: p.53
© The Royal Society: pp.74 (top), 75 (top), 80 (top)
Courtesy of the Marquess of Salisbury: p.31
Courtesy of the Shakespeare Birthplace Trust: p.50 (top)
© Nick Sinclair p.13
Cecil Beaton photograph courtesy of Sotheby's London: p.134 (left)
© Sotheby's: p.101 (bottom)
Lord Snowdon, Vogue 1981 © Condé Nast Publications Ltd: p.157
© John Swannell: p.12 (centre), 159 (right)
© Tate, London 2002: pp. 24, 68–9, 79
By kind permission of the Marquess of Tavistock and the Trustees of the Bedford Estates: p.36 (bottom)
© Mario Testino: pp.25, 152–3
By kind permission of the Masters and Fellows of Trinity College, Cambridge, p.78 (top)
Courtesy Universal Pictures/Miramax films/RGA: p.44
Courtesy of the Trustees of the V&A/Mike Kitcatt: p.36 (top)
Courtesy of the Trustees of the V&A/ Mr D. P. P. Naish: p.37 (left)
The Wellcome Library, London: p.77
© Robert Whitaker: p.145 (top right), 149
By kind permission of Mr J. K. Wingfield Digby: pp.24, 26–7 (detail)

One hundred heroes and more
BY MARK HARRISON

Mario Testino signing copies of his book at the National Portrait Gallery exhibition
Photograph, 560 × 178mm (22 × 7″)
David Weightman, 2002

A. J. P. Taylor (1906–90) and Simon Schama
Courtesy of BBC Picture Archives

Cliff Richard
Derek Allen, 1958
Modern bromide print from original negative, 283 × 222mm (11⅛ × 8¾″)
National Portrait Gallery, London (NPG x45957)

Bob Geldof
John Swannell, 1989
Iris print, 494 × 394mm (19½ × 15½″)
National Portrait Gallery, London (NPG P717(7))

Robbie Williams
Hamish Brown, 1998
Bromide fibre print, 460 × 335mm (18¾ × 13¼″)
National Portrait Gallery, London (NPG x87829)

William Wilberforce
Sir Thomas Lawrence, 1828
Oil on canvas, 965 × 1092mm (38 × 43″)
National Portrait Gallery, London (NPG 3)

Enoch Powell
Nick Sinclair, 1992
Bromide print, 376 × 291mm (14¾ × 11⅜″)
National Portrait Gallery, London (NPG P563(31))

John Keats
William Hilton after Joseph Severn, c.1822
Oil on canvas, 762 × 635mm (30 × 25″)
National Portrait Gallery, London (NPG 194)

John Constable
Self-portrait, c.1779–1804
Pencil and black chalk heightened with white and red chalk, 248 × 194mm (9¾ × 7⅝″)
National Portrait Gallery, London (NPG 901)

The Hay Wain
John Constable, 1821
Oil on canvas, 1302 × 1854mm (51¼ × 73″)
National Gallery, London

The Tudor Galleries, Ondaatje Wing
Andrew Putler, 2001
National Portrait Gallery, London

Why biography matters to us
BY BRIAN HARRISON

Newspaper cutting
Daily Express, October 27, 1965

Talvin Singh receiving the Mercury Music Prize, 2000

Sir Oswald Mosley addressing a meeting at Victoria Park Square, Bethnal Green, London, 14 October, 1934
National Portrait Gallery, London (RN 25681)

Samuel Johnson
James Barry, c.1778–80
Oil on canvas, 606 × 530mm (23⅞ × 20⅞″)
National Portrait Gallery, London (NPG 1185)

Virginia Woolf
George Charles Beresford, 1902
Platinum print, 152 × 108mm (6 × 4¼″)
National Portrait Gallery, London (NPG P221)

National Portrait Gallery, London. Exterior View.

Researchers working on the Dictionary of National Biography

Index

Figures in italic refer to illustrations.

Contributors

ROSIE BOYCOTT

Rosie Boycott was a founder of the feminist magazine *Spare Rib* and of Virago Publishing. She was the first woman in Britain to edit a broadsheet newspaper and to edit a daily paper, and has been the Editor of *Spare Rib*, the *Independent on Sunday*, the *Independent*, the *Daily Express* and the *Sunday Express*. She has published several books including a novel and a volume of autobiography. She makes regular appearances on television and radio programmes, including Radio Four's *Start the Week*, *Question Time* and *Any Questions*.

JEREMY CLARKSON

Jeremy Clarkson trained as a journalist on the *Rotherham Advertiser*. After working as a local news reporter (and a stint in the family business, selling Paddington Bears), he coupled his writing skills with his interest in cars and formed the Motoring Press Agency in 1984. His television career started with the motoring programme, *Top Gear*, which was followed by programmes on travel and engineering and machine-related topics. He writes weekly columns in the *Sunday Times* and the *Sun* and contributes to *Top Gear* magazine, and has had several books published.

JOHN COOPER

After five years in teaching, John became Education Officer and then Head of Education at the National Army Museum. He was Head of Education at the National Portrait Gallery, London, from 1981 until his retirement in 2001. He continues to write and lecture for the Gallery, and is working on a novel set in eighteenth-century London.

ALAN DAVIES

Alan Davies is one of Britain's best-known stand-up comics. After appearing on Jo Brand's *Through the Cakehole*, he made his name on *Have I Got News for You*, where he guest starred between 1995 and 1997. Television drama roles include *One for the Road* (1995), *Jonathan Creek* (1997), for which he was named most popular actor in the 1998 National TV awards, and *Bob and Rose* (2001). He was named best young comic in the 1991 *Time Out* awards and nominated as best stand-up comic at the 1995 British Comedy Awards.

BRIAN HARRISON

Brian Harrison is Professor of Modern British History at Oxford University, and has been Editor of the *New Dictionary of National Biography* since January 2000. His books include *Drink and the Victorians. The Temperance Question in England 1815–1872* (1971), *Prudent Revolutionaries. Portraits of British Feminists between the Wars* (1987), and *The Transformation of British Politics 1860–1995* (1996).

MARK HARRISON

Mark Harrison is Series Producer of *Great Britons* for the BBC. He began his career as a research fellow in history at King's College, Cambridge. Since moving into television, he has produced and directed over 100 programmes, ranging from *Visions of Heaven and Hell* and *Break up* for Channel Four to *Three Minute Culture*, *Comic Relief* and *Century Road* for the BBC.

RICHARD HOLMES

Richard Holmes is Professor of Military and Security Studies at Cranfield University. His many books include *Redcoat: The British Soldier in the Age of Horse and Musket*. He has presented a number of historical documentaries, including *War Walks* and, most recently, a series on the Duke of Wellington.

TRISTRAM HUNT

Dr Tristram Hunt is an associate fellow at the Centre for History and Economics, Cambridge. He read history at Trinity College, Cambridge and the University of Chicago. His doctoral thesis is the basis for his forthcoming book, *Building Jerusalem: The Victorian City from Liverpool to Letchworth* (Weidenfeld & Nicolson, 2003). He writes regularly for the *Guardian* and recently wrote and presented a television series on the English Civil War.

ANDREW MARR

Andrew Marr has been the BBC Political Editor since May 2000. He joined *The Scotsman* as a trainee in 1981 and became its parliamentary correspondent in 1984, returning there in 1986 as Political Editor. He has also worked at the *Independent* (where he was promoted to Editor in 1996) and *The Economist*, and as a columnist for the *Daily Express* and the *Observer*. He has received several awards, including Columnist of the Year in both the British Press Awards and the What the Papers Say awards for 1995. His most recent book is *The Day Britain Died* (Profile, 2000).

MARJORIE (MO) MOWLAM

Dr Mo Mowlam was a member of the UK Government and Tony Blair's Cabinet until the General Election of June 2001. She has been Secretary of State for Northern Ireland and later Minister for the Cabinet Office and Chancellor of the Duchy of Lancaster. Her political memoir, *Momentum*, was published in May 2002. She is a member of the International Conflict Group and spends much of her free time raising money for charities.

LUCY MOORE

Lucy Moore read history at Edinburgh University. She is the author of the critically acclaimed *The Thieves' Opera: The Remarkable Lives and Deaths of Jonathan Wild, Thief-Taker, and Jack Sheppard, House-Breaker* (Viking, 1997) and *Amphibious Thing: The Life of a Georgian Rake* (Viking, 2000). She is currently writing, *Maharanis: The Lives and Times of Three Generations of Indian Queens* which will be published in 2004. Her television documentaries include *When Money Went Mad: The Story of the South Sea Bubble* for Channel Four (2000).

MICHAEL PORTILLO

Michael Portillo has been in Parliament for a total of fifteen years, and rose to be Secretary of State for Defence. Recently he has devoted time to making films for television, including *A Great Railway Journey* (a biographical sketch of his father) and *Art That Shook the World: Richard Wagner's 'Ring'*.

FIONA SHAW

Fiona Shaw studied at the Royal Academy of Dramatic Art and has worked extensively at the National Theatre. Since her 1989 movie debut in *My Left Foot* she has also co-starred in nine films, including *The Butcher Boy* (1997) and *Three Men and a Little Lady* (1990). She has won three Laurence Olivier Awards for Best Actress, and she was awarded an Officier des Arts et Lettres in France in 2000 and an honorary CBE in the 2001 New Year's Honours List.